D1491093

CREATE IN ME
A PURE HEART

ANSWERS FOR STRUGGLING WOMEN

STEVE & KATHY
GALLAGHER

CREATE IN ME A PURE HEART

ANSWERS FOR STRUGGLING WOMEN

www.purelifeministries.org

888.PURELIFE

ADVANCE PRAISE FOR CREATE IN ME A PURE HEART

"Here's a heartfelt thanks to Steve and Kathy Gallagher for writing, *Create In Me A Pure Heart*. This book will be a comfort and a help to so many women who struggle with sexual sin…and have felt isolated for far too long. Intentional steps are provided to guide to a place of hope and healing. The challenge to pray, 'Lord, change me from the inside out." is the central point of this book. For this, we applaud Steve and Kathy as they point women to God as the only answer for life's challenges."

> CLAY AND RENEE CROSSE
> HOLYHOMES.ORG

"*Create in Me A Pure Heart* is a straightforward, raw and urgent call to holiness. It is a powerful compilation of research, Scripture, and real life stories of both struggle and freedom. This book is invaluable for every shamed captive daughter who has ever wanted true empowerment as well as for every counselor or pastor who's wondered how to approach this growing problem."

> LISA BEVERE
> BESTSELLING AUTHOR OF *Kissed the Girls and Made Them Cry*

"You or someone you love may be caught in this trap and think there is no way out, but I have good news for you—this book is not a concept of freedom, but truly a roadmap to freedom. I wish every human being on the planet would take the time to read this book!"

> NANCY ALCORN
> FOUNDER OF MERCY MINISTRIES

"*Create in Me a Pure Heart* is much needed! This book will be a 'must have' for our ministry."

> CRAIG GROSS
> FOUNDER OF XXXCHURCH.COM

"Once again, Steve and Kathy Gallagher are on the cutting edge of an emerging issue. As they point out in their ground-breaking book, *Create in Me a Pure Heart*, women are becoming trapped in pornography and sexual sin in alarming numbers. Not only does this book describe the deep shame and struggle these women face, but it also provides a clearly defined path back to purity and hope for deliverance."

BEVERLY LAHAYE,
CONCERNED WOMEN FOR AMERICA

"A must read for every woman whose life has been stained by past or present sexual sin. With compassion and truth, Steve and Kathy Gallagher boldly take you to the root of your issues. As a woman who has walked this path of sexual sin, and now walks with Christ alone, I can assure you that this is one resource the enemy does not want you to have on your spiritual journey."

CARMEN PATE,
CO-HOST, *Point of View Talk Show*

"Too often the root problem is never understood and therefore never addressed, thus keeping the enslaved without hope for freedom. But this book offers great hope for deliverance because it clearly exposes the root problem and shows the way to lasting freedom. I recommend it as a 'must read' for anyone seeking freedom."

DR. RUTH RUIBAL,
MISSIONARY, CALI, COLOMBIA

"Steve and Kathy unmask the spirit of this world that promises pleasure but delivers bondage. This book will help you to recognize the lies that allure women into the snare of sexual addiction and empower you to live free from enslavement to sin. Living in victory is possible!"

MERCY HOPE,
INTERVIEWER, FAITHTALKS.COM

ALSO AVAILABLE BY STEVE GALLAGHER:

At the Altar of Sexual Idolatry
At the Altar of Sexual Idolatry Workbook
A Biblical Guide to Counseling the Sexual Addict
How America Lost Her Innocence
Intoxicated with Babylon
Irresistible to God
A Lamp Unto My Feet
Living in Victory
Out of the Depths of Sexual Sin
Pressing On Toward the Heavenly Calling
The Walk of Repentance

For these books and other teaching materials please contact:

PURE LIFE MINISTRIES
14 School Street
Dry Ridge, KY 41035
(888) PURELIFE - to order
(859) 824-4444
(859) 813-0005 FAX
www.purelifeministries.org

CREATE IN ME A PURE HEART
Copyright © 2007 by Steve and Kathy Gallagher.
All rights reserved. No part of this book may be reproduced
in any form except for brief quotations, without
written permission from the author.

ISBN 0-9758832-7-5
EAN 978-0-9758832-7-3

Unless otherwise noted, Scripture quotations taken from the
NEW AMERICAN STANDARD BIBLE,
Copyright © 1960, 1962, 1963, 1968, 1971, 1972, 1973, 1975, 1977, 1995,
by The Lockman Foundation. Used by permission. (www.Lockman.org)

VISIT THE CREATE IN ME A PURE HEART BLOG

and Journal Your Thoughts as You Read

∽҉⊹∾

We have created a special blog for this book. Its purpose is to be a place for you to share what the Lord is doing in your life as you read. Each chapter will have posts by Kathy Gallagher, as well as links to free resources that will further minister to you. Stop by to post your own thoughts or to just read what others are saying for your own encouragement. Either way, it's there for you at:

www.purelifeministries.org/pureheartblog

ACKNOWLEDGMENTS

We would like to thank all of the women who participated in the Pure Life Ministries website survey. The stories you shared painted a vivid picture of what many other women are quietly facing alone.

We would also like to thank Ed and Karla Buch, Judy Asmus, Michelle and Ashley Hensley, Judy Lucas and Rose Colón for their valuable input.

DEDICATION

*We dedicate this book to all of the struggling women
who are determined to fight for a holy life in God.
May the Lord abundantly answer your cry
for a pure heart!*

CONTENTS

INTRODUCTION

A Note from Kathy to the Reader

My husband's book, *At the Altar of Sexual Idolatry* was written by a man to men in the throes of sexual addiction. At times it is a very hard-hitting book. Steve takes aim at the underlying motives that have made a way for a Christian man to indulge himself in sexual sin. In spite of that, there is a reason that there are over 150,000 copies in print. As painful as it can be to read at times, men understand that this book is packed with sound, biblical truth and the God-given answer to habitual sin. That's why it breathes hope to the reader throughout.

The first three chapters of *Create in Me a Pure Heart* are completely new, written to the Christian woman who struggles with sexual sin. Chapters Four through Seventeen are an adaptation of *At the Altar of Sexual Idolatry*, rewritten to apply to women.

As Steve's wife I know better than anybody what a deeply loving man he truly is. The staff of Pure Life Ministries understands this as well. Part of his no-nonsense approach is simply because he tends to be that way by nature. But there is also the aspect that he really hates the sin that ruins lives, destroys families and corrupts the Body of Christ.

There will be times as you go through this book that some

truth about yourself will hit you so hard that you may want to set the book down for a few days. That's okay! Please don't let hurt feelings prevent you from getting what you need. God wants to set you abundantly free, but there will be times when the process will be painful. Those who insist on having "feel-good" solutions wrapped in emotional rhetoric and placating jargon will never find freedom.

I pray that as you read this book, you will find the liberating power of the Holy Spirit there to help you through the process of finding the true and lasting freedom you desire.

GOD BLESS YOU,
KATHY GALLAGHER

CREATE IN ME A PURE HEART

Part 1: THE PROBLEM

CHAPTER ONE:
WOMEN AND SEXUAL SIN

*"She who gives herself to wanton pleasure
is dead even while she lives." (I Timothy 5:6)*

"I became so obsessed with getting the attention of men," recounts Beth, "that I would actually try to charm married men into thinking I was more wonderful than their wives. How sick is that?"*

Susan's husband introduced her to X-rated movies, but—as we will soon see—it wasn't long before she developed her own infatuation with the adult entertainment industry.

Lisa wasn't promiscuous, but she so craved the attention of men that she would purposely wear revealing clothes—even in church.

Tiffany was a 14-year-old pastor's daughter who got involved in sexual conversations in chat rooms. She finally became involved in an Internet romance. "It was beautiful for me, because I didn't have to give him my body in return."

To the people around her at church, Jane seemed like a typical Christian woman, but she assumed a different persona during her weekly trips to other cities.

---

* Nearly all of the stories provided in this book are real. The others are composites of people we have dealt with over the years. Pseudonyms are used to protect the privacy of those involved.

The behavior of all of these women varied, but they each shared two things in common: they were all professing Christians and they all used sexual sin to gratify themselves.

While there are those women who are simply addicted to some type of sexual activity, most women involved in illicit sex use it as a means to attain some deeper form of satisfaction, such as the desire to feel loved, be noticed, or even be desired sexually. Many women start down the road simply looking for attention or fulfillment but end up addicted to some form of sexual behavior.

For Christians, sexual sin always brings with it a sense of guilt and shame. This creates a tension between a driving sexual lust and the desire to live a life pleasing to God. The following is an email which came in to the Pure Life Ministries website that really shows the pain and desperation churchgoing women experience when sex takes hold of their minds.

> I am very overwhelmed by my sin of distorted sexual fantasies which lead me to masturbation. I also am weary of fighting intense lustful thoughts, with almost any guy around me, younger or older. I have been alternately fighting and not fighting for many years now and am tired and scared of myself. I do not know if other girls struggle like this, but my urges and desires are so strong. I just need help. I am so fearful that the reason I am not married is because God is punishing me for these impure thoughts, and honestly, I don't know that any guy would satisfy me because I want sex so badly, or that any guy would want to be with me because I think such disgusting thoughts. I am so weary and have failed so miserably to have self-control in this area.
>
> How can God keep forgiving me if I keep willfully sinning? How can I live a life honoring God and helping others if I am plagued by such debilitating sin? How can

I set a good example for my students if I'm as full of lust as they are? How abnormal am I, as a woman, to be fighting with this? Is there any hope? Sometimes I'd rather be dead and in heaven with Christ than continue to fail like this; yet the desires are so strong.

The truth is that Christian women are not only becoming increasingly involved in traditional forms of sexual sin such as fornication and adultery, but are now branching out into new activities such as lesbianism and cyber-sex. For instance, consider the following statistics about the online activities of women:

- Women are twice as likely as men to visit chat rooms.[1]
- One out of every six Christian women is addicted to pornography or another form of sexual sin.[2]
- 28% of visitors to adult websites are female.[3]

Are these numbers truly accurate? We don't know for certain. What *is* clear to us is that Christian women are indulging in sexual sin like never before.

Desiring to get a sense of exactly what female evangelicals are struggling with, we recently conducted a survey through the Pure Life Ministries website in which nearly 500 women (who acknowledged having struggled with sexual sin) participated.** We addressed three primary categories with our questions: romance, pornography and sexual activity. Here are three of the questions and their results:

1. Which of the following types of behavior regarding romance, past or present, have you been involved in? Select all that apply.

** For the complete results of this survey, along with a breakdown of age groups, please see Addendum, page 261.

    a. Entertaining romantic fantasies: 72%
    b. Reading romance novels: 29%
    c. Watching soap operas: 23%
    d. Establishing romantic relationships on the Internet: 18%
    e. Flirting with guys: 40%
    f. Frequent casual dating: 14%
    g. Watching romantic movies: 53%

2. Which of the following types of behavior regarding pornography, past or present, have you been involved in? Select all that apply.
    a. Viewing adult movies with another person: 29%
    b. Viewing adult movies alone: 44%
    c. Occasionally viewing magazines/Internet pornography: 53%
    d. Regularly viewing magazines/Internet pornography: 19%
    e. Reading pornographic stories: 46%

3. Which of the following types of behavior regarding sexual sin, past or present, have you been involved in? Select all that apply.
    a. Masturbation: 90%
    b. Online sexual conversations: 31%
    c. Promiscuity/fornication with other singles: 36%
    d. Affair(s): 12%
    e. Straight but having bisexual experiences: 15%
    f. Homosexual lifestyle: 3%
    g. Involved in the adult entertainment industry: 4%

Keep in mind that these are women who acknowledged struggling with sexual sin and these results should not be applied to the female Christian population at large. However, they do clearly reflect the fact that many evangelical women are dealing with a variety of different types of sexual sin.

Viewing Adult Entertainment

Susan's face betrayed her disgust the first time her husband suggested they watch an adult movie together. "Honey, not only will it enhance our lovemaking," Jim exclaimed, "but I won't need to have a sex life apart from you. It will end all the sneaking around."

She had long since given up hope of him quitting his online addiction, but this was too much. "We are Christians, Jim," she protested, "and this is wrong!"

"*Wrong?*" Jim argued. "I know of Christian therapists who suggest couples use it to improve their sex lives. How can it be wrong?"

After years of dealing with Jim's secret sex life, Susan eventually acquiesced and joined what is becoming an ever-increasing number of Christian women who regularly view pornography. This phenomenon bucks the customary notion that it is only men who are visually stimulated and thereby more prone to viewing porn. Traditionally, women have been far more likely to engage in wistful, romantic fantasies rather than watching lewd scenes of people engaging in sexual acts. However, over the past few years a disturbing new trend has emerged: *women viewing pornography in alarming numbers.*

To illustrate, Nielsen NetRatings reports that nearly one-third of the visitors to adult websites are female. They estimate that 9.4 million women in the United States accessed online pornography in September 2003.[4]

Jim introducing Susan to the world of adult entertainment is typical of how most females become involved. The first time he brought home a movie, she was shocked at what she saw. It was so revolting to her that she tried to ignore the scenes being played out on their bedroom television set, instead focusing her attention on her husband. As for Jim, she had never seen him so passionate toward her. It was thrilling! Susan grappled with what she had done over the next few days, vacillating between guilt and excitement. In the end, she made a conscious decision that she was willing to exchange her self-respect for his affection.

Just as Jim had promised, there was a heightened level of excitement in their intimacy that hadn't been there since their wedding night many years before. Once she got past the initial shock of the explicitness, she actually came to look forward to their "special times" on Saturday nights. The intense pleasure of these experiences gave them something they could share together.

One thing that was a bit surprising to Susan was the quality of the videos. They weren't the cheaply produced films she had come to expect. The world of adult entertainment had its own producers, directors, camera crews, stars and starlets. Everything was topnotch. Over time, Susan began to not only enjoy the effects of the movies on their sex life but the movies themselves. While Jim was fascinated with body parts and explicit scenes, Susan was drawn to the seductive storylines and her favorite actors—and actresses. Yes, a *lust for women* had been kindled within her.

Their relationship seemed idyllic those first few weeks. Although Susan had to silence her guilty conscience and stifle her nagging concerns, she and Jim got along better than ever before. But, as we all know, the pleasure of sin only lasts for a season. Unbeknownst to her, a very evil, corrupting influence had been loosed deep within her being. The "sex-is-everything" mindset communicated by these motion pictures began to break down many of her inhibitions. She found herself fantasizing about other men—and women. Sometimes she even secretly watched the movies by herself while Jim was at work.

There was another troubling development occurring as well.

Their relationship, which had become full of tenderness and devotion, began to deteriorate. Jim became more distant than ever, causing Susan to become suspicious and argumentative. They squabbled over petty differences. What's more, when they were out in public, Jim openly gawked at every pretty girl he saw. How could Susan scold him, after what she had allowed into their home? Little by little things became worse, until finally, Jim left and Susan filed for divorce. Now, as a middle-aged woman with a failed marriage, the loss of her self-respect and the hollowness of soul that porn produces, she was more miserable than ever.

This case is fairly typical of what occurs when wives allow pornography to be brought into the home. As the number of Christian men addicted to porn continues to increase, it can be expected that the number of wives and girlfriends involved will also grow.

Online Pornography

However, there is another disturbing trend that is also emerging: women who are seeking out pornography for themselves.

One such person was Julie, a serious-minded, young businesswoman. Like Susan, before becoming involved in porn, Julie's life would have been considered normal by today's Christian standards. Although involved with the singles group of her church, she struggled with feelings of loneliness. Julie secretly envied the "bubbly" girls in the group who always seemed to attract the guys. Sometimes she despaired of ever finding "Mr. Right." For some time she had been watching one of the leading network soap operas, allowing the immorality portrayed on the show to fuel her secret fantasy of being a beautiful seductress.

She was embarrassed one evening when the pastor's wife

came for an unexpected visit while the show she had recorded that day was playing on her TV set. The older woman's face flushed when she saw a torrid love scene being enacted on the screen. Julie's feigned indignation masked the fact that she had come to enjoy this kind of fare. The truth was that she continually fostered romantic and sexual fantasies about a number of male acquaintances at her job.

Another pastime unexpectedly developed in Julie's life. One day, she confided her struggles with loneliness to a girlfriend from church. Her friend suggested she visit Christian chat rooms on the Internet where she could develop risk-free relationships with men. At first, she tried it hesitantly and carefully, but before long she was heavily involved. Eventually, she expanded her involvement to include larger, secular chat rooms. Initially, the amount of sexual talk alarmed her, but she gradually became fascinated with it. Of course, anytime she posted a message, she would be swarmed by interested men. It was almost like being a starlet in her own soap opera!

Occasionally, Julie would come across messages that advertised adult websites. In the beginning, she resisted her curiosity about them, but she finally got to the place where she had no resistance left. One night she impulsively clicked on a link to an adult website. She panicked when an image of a copulating couple popped up on the screen, quickly closing the site with trembling hands. But that scene haunted her memory until, a few nights later, she revisited the site. She was so enthralled by what she saw that she was completely drawn in. After the exhilaration of that night, her soap opera seemed tame and boring. She found herself returning to the adult websites time and again. She knew what she was doing was wrong but, despite repeated promises to quit her behavior, she kept going back to it. This young lady, who had once been shy and naïve, had completely corrupted herself with a thorough knowledge of evil.

Cyber-Sex

Christy was introduced to the Internet while still in middle school. She was instantly addicted. "I was an awkward young girl," she recalls with a painful expression. "I was full of love and life, but I was overweight and ashamed of the way I looked. While my brothers and sisters were all overachievers, I felt ugly and mediocre—a disappointment to my family."

It wasn't long before the young girl began exploring chat rooms that focused on theater and music. "I liked who I was online. I felt safe behind the screen because no one could see me. It was a thrill to meet people who said they liked me."

Although she was only 13-years-old, Christy told her online acquaintances that she was 17 or 18. She soon began meeting guys who were in that age range—or at least that's what they told her. Over the next couple of years she started forming strong, unhealthy relationships with these online personalities. Every day she would be on the computer, visiting chat rooms and instant-messaging with guys she met.

Eventually, she became involved with a 27-year-old guy from Chicago. They carried on an intense online relationship which carried over into phone calls. She tells what happened next:

> Jim loved my speaking voice. I remember feeling so sexy on the phone, covering up my age and speaking maturely. This man began to fall in love with me. We talked daily, flirtatiously and romantically. He constantly told me things like I was beautiful, smart or funny.
>
> Late one night, we began instant-messaging and our conversation turned very flirtatious. He began to tell me things he'd like to do with me if we ever met. Our flirting turned into heated sexual conversation. I'd watched pornography before, but there was something so much more thrilling about reading his words and

knowing that it was me who turned him on.

After that, we began talking long distance more and more. Our phone sex got graphic, and I began to get good at it. I knew what turned him on and often led the conversations.

Jim became obsessed with me and the idea of us getting together. He constantly talked about driving to my hometown to visit me. He thought I was 18-years-old and on my way to college. I would continually make excuses why we could not see each other but never told him the truth about my age or appearance.

Jim didn't know that while I was carrying on with him I was also involved with six other guys. I had cyber-sex with all of them. In fact, I was the one who initiated it most of the time. I loved the fact that they all seemed desperate to have me. Each one of them wanted to meet me, even offering to pay to visit me. During this time, I totally lost myself. I was lying to so many people that I had a hard time distinguishing what was reality. It was not just about sex, but about the romance, the attention, the compliments and the intrigue of meeting new people.

Eventually, I came to the Lord and began to end these relationships. When I told Jim how old I was and that I couldn't continue the relationship, he was heartbroken and then became so irate that I had to hang up the phone on him.

Not long after this, while sitting in my freshman social studies class, I got a call from the office that I was being checked out of school. I panicked, thinking it was my mom and that something had happened to one of my family members.

When I walked in the hall, there was Jim, who had driven all the way from Chicago. Somehow he figured out what school I attended. I darted out the door and hid in the bathroom, shaking violently. After school was out, I waited until everyone had left and ran home, cutting through yards and houses, like a frightened criminal.

Addicted to a Sexual High

Jill's problems began in 7th grade when Denny Schmidt asked her to dance. Since she had a crush on him she was elated. As their bodies fused together to the slow rhythms of the Righteous Brothers, a powerful feeling of sensuality surged through her body. She was instantly addicted to this new sensation. From that point on Jill began looking for opportunities to be alone with boys so they could "make out."

During her teen years Jill appeared to be a good Christian girl. She would go to prayer meetings, play the piano for church meetings and even attend Youth for Christ meetings on Saturday nights. "Through all of this," she remembers, "I was involved in the church. I sang in girl's ensembles, the church choir, was on Bible quiz teams and began playing the organ in church. I had deceived myself into believing that I was okay with the Lord. I can even remember sitting at a swimming pool playing cards and telling a guy how he needed Jesus. It seemed I equated being a fisher of men with salvation. I didn't realize how I was grieving the Holy Spirit. I often prayed for God to protect me from getting pregnant, but I don't recall ever praying to be set free."

By 10th grade, her sexual encounters progressed from petting to intercourse. There were even times she would leave a Youth for Christ meeting on Saturday night to go have sex with her boyfriend.

When she entered college, she decided that she should find a guy who she could marry. She settled on a young man named William. He was a handsome guy who came from an affluent family. Jill was able to win his affections and it wasn't long before the two were married. There was only one problem: he wasn't a passionate lover. In fact, William wasn't all that interested in sex. "Since our sex life wasn't very good, I started coming on to other men," she recalls.

One of these men Jill enticed was her best friend's husband. Soon the two of them began a passionate affair. Eventually they told their mates and set out on their own. But having a man who enjoyed sex just as much as she did brought no more satisfaction than anything else she had done. Before long the two went their individual ways—both of their marriages destroyed in the process.

Now, Jill became so obsessed with sex that she would do practically anything to get a man in bed. "I became a seductress," she says. When she was 27-years-old, she seduced a 17-year-old boy who lived nearby. "No matter who I managed to get into bed, I had absolutely NO peace," she exclaims. "I was in a constant state of agitation. Nothing brought relief from the inner misery I felt. I hated the feeling I had after sex. I had never disliked myself in high school and college. I was always upbeat and confident, but now I felt cheap and dirty. I was disgusted with what I had become."

One particularly painful day, the frustration of her life came boiling out. She started pacing back and forth in the house yelling, "I'm addicted to sex! I'm addicted to sex! What am I going to do? I can't live without a man!"

Same-Sex Attraction

Stacey was actually engaged to be married when she decided that she was "gay." She arrived at this conclusion primarily as a result of the growing anxiety she was experiencing over her impending honeymoon. Of course, the thought of having sex for the first time is enough to cause any young virgin to be nervous. But in Stacey's case, there was the added element that she was marrying a man she simply did not love. John was her best friend and the two had gone steady for six years, but there was nothing about him that aroused her passions. She assumed that since she dreaded the thought of having sex with him there must be something wrong with her.

At the same time she was struggling with this issue, she happened to meet a lesbian at her job. The two became close friends and one day Stacey confessed to her that she thought she might be gay. She was relieved to have someone she could finally open up to about the struggles she was going through. The more the two discussed her situation, the more convinced she became that she was actually a "closet" homosexual. Before it was over, the two girls kissed. The excitement she felt in that moment of passion was the final confirmation she needed.

Now that it was settled in her heart that she was actually homosexual, Stacey broke off her engagement. This gave her the freedom to visit a gay bar. The first time she walked in, she discovered that she was the only girl there wearing a dress. Because she had always been very feminine, she instantly stood out to every lesbian in the place. They showered her with affection that night. "I felt like I was the prettiest girl in the whole world," she recalls. "I liked that feeling!"

Before long she had entered into a monogamous relationship with one of the lesbians who frequented the bar. Although the two of them ended up living together for seven years, they quit having sex within the first two years. Stacey actually lost interest in the sex but enjoyed the emotional connection the two shared.

Eventually she came under conviction about her lifestyle and repented. Today Stacey is happily married to a man she truly loves—and enjoys.

Stacey is part of another growing segment within our culture: straight girls who are turning to bisexuality for satisfaction.

According to a report by the U.S. Centers for Disease Control and Prevention, more women are experimenting with homosexual activity than ever before. The report found that 11% of women they surveyed had had a sexual experience with another woman, compared with only 4% in a similar 1992 survey.

Younger women, however, were even more likely to dabble in homosexuality. According to an article in the Washington Post, 14% of women in their late teens and 20's claimed to have had a same-sex experience.[5]

Some experts said an increasing number of young people simply see such experimentation as a rite of passage: "It's very safe in the academic community; no one thinks anything of it," Elayne Rapping, a professor of American Studies at the University of Buffalo, told the Post.[6]

In fact, the article continues, lesbian experimentation, even among heterosexual women, has become so chic on campuses that some jokingly refer to being "lesbian until graduation," or "LUG," according to Craig Kinsley, a neuroscientist at the University of Richmond.[7]

While much of this phenomenon can be chalked up to the widespread acceptance of homosexuality within our culture, another aspect of it is simply that many women feel that it is possible to have an emotional connection with another woman that they don't believe they can achieve with a man. This emotional connection is not only at the root of much of the bisexual experimentation that is going on, but it also contributes to many other forms of sexual sin women participate in.

CHAPTER TWO:
ROMANCE AND THE
EMOTIONAL CONNECTION

*"Those who belong to Christ have crucified their
old nature with all that it loved and lusted for."
(Galatians 5:24 PHP)*

I t was early 2005, and for a time we (Steve & Kathy) lived in
Eastern Kentucky, about 2½ hours away from the Pure Life
Ministries facility. One day, we visited a Christian bookstore
and found a novel on CD that we hoped would provide a break
from the tedium of a weekly drive that had become all too
familiar.

The authoress had written a series of books which revolved
around a family of orphans who had grown to adulthood
together. This particular story began with an exciting sequence
of events that led into a whodunit mystery. Woven through this
gripping storyline was the budding romance between the heroine
and her older stepbrother's best friend. The personalities of
these two characters gradually emerged as the story unfolded.
The man was rugged, handsome and extremely sensitive to the
young woman's needs. She was feisty and cantankerous—all of
which he handled with the greatest patience and tenderness.
Before long it became obvious that the woman who had written
this novel was projecting her idea of the perfect male into this
man's character. No matter what the woman did to push him

away, he always treated her with the utmost amount of love and tenderness. Once we realized how she was propagating romantic fantasy, we threw the CD's away.

While we were repulsed by her characterizations, the success of this series of books shows that there are plenty of women who thoroughly enjoyed them. What can account for this success? Undoubtedly, it is the fact that the storyline appeals to a fantasy which nearly every woman entertains at some point: Prince Charming rides into her life, rescues her from the villain (because, after all, her hero can't be a wimp!) and through it all, showers her with love and affection.

One would expect young women and even teenagers to deal with such fantasies, but amazingly, this is a mindset that becomes entrenched even in younger girls. Consider the fascinating story of Tiffany, now a 19-year-old virgin who has never even kissed a guy. Her father is a devout pastor who went through great pains to protect his kids from unholy influences. In spite of the godly leadership she received at home, she came close to disaster in a completely unforeseeable way. Believe it or not, it all began with watching animated movies. As she asks, "Where do you think this generation's young women have developed such unrealistic expectations about some perfect, handsome prince saving them from all their troubles?" Even animated movies typically revolve around some version of Prince Charming and the damsel in distress. We'll let Tiffany tell in her own words how this imaginary fairytale started her down the wrong road in her mind—and where that road took her.

> Those kinds of scenarios [from animated movies] were permanently etched into my mind. I remember many times, even when I was 8, 9, or 10 years of age, taking myself and whoever I "liked" for the week and placing us together in that picture perfect place: on that horse, boat, or grassy field, holding each other, and

confessing our love for one another. My thoughts were already headed desperately in the wrong direction. By the time I was 12, my thought life was out of control. I had, in my mind, married at least 20 different people. I had at least 6 different honeymoon destinations. Every minute of the day I was thinking about marriage. I grew up in church, and so I knew sex before marriage was wrong. I made sure all of my fantasies came complete with a wedding. I would daydream for long periods of time about different boys whom I thought would be suitable husbands and the incredible lengths they would go to in order to win my love.

I began masturbating when I was 8, but consistently by the age of 10. I wanted an emotional relationship with a boy. I wanted that deep connection. In my fantasy, it wasn't enough anymore just to be together, it had to be more. I would picture the series of events leading up to the sexual liaison: the hugging, kissing, being close. It wasn't about body parts, it was about connection. No one showed me how to masturbate; in fact I did not even know what it was called. I just started one night when I was thinking about some romantic situation, and because of my sin nature, it came, well, naturally.

There was a time that I remember saying in my heart, "God, You can't fulfill this part of my life. You can't meet this need. This is too deep, too big, too wide for You." And that is exactly how I felt. It was the lie I believed. I was looking at my Creator and my body, and telling Him that He could not satisfy me. That lie was the crux of my sin.

By the time I was 14, I started getting involved in the Internet and eventually exploring chat rooms. I had Internet relationships with 5 different guys. But "JesseJames" was the one I would fall "in love" with.

One night he instant-messaged me outside one of the filthy chat rooms I was visiting, and we began what you could call an "Internet romance."

At first our conversations were harmless: music, books, movies, etc. Then things went deeper. I shared everything with him. It was a romance. I fell in love with who he was, or who he made himself out to be, and it was beautiful for me, because I didn't have to give him my body in return.

After about 3 weeks our emails became increasingly long and frequent, and we started talking about our "feelings" for one another. By then he was asking me about my bedroom, undergarments and so on. I would answer innocently and reluctantly. I did not want to refuse him and lose his companionship.

One night he asked me if we would ever meet. I knew it would be wrong, but in my blindness I agreed to plan a rendezvous at a swank local restaurant. To me this was it. I knew in my heart that if we met I would have to give something to him. I had gotten to the point where I was willing to go that far for his affection.

But God, just in time, exposed my sin. As I was emailing him one night, my Dad walked right into my room, asked me who I was emailing, and it was over. He sat at my computer and read out loud every single email that we had written—as I sat there and sobbed. My sin, not in its entirety, but the outward manifestation of it, was exposed. God had uncovered that area in my life, and that is where the healing started.

Not every girl who gives over to romantic fantasies ends up in an online sexual relationship, but there is no question that giving oneself over to that thinking opens the door for other problems.

For most girls, this fairytale thinking about romance begins by daydreaming about some guy at school. Take Robin, for instance. She is a 17-year-old girl who attends a Christian school. She developed a crush on a cute guy named Josh. She could easily spend hours daydreaming about him: his smile, his blue eyes, his dimples. Over and over she would replay those thoughts in her mind. One day, the two came across each other in the school parking lot and for a nanosecond (an eternal moment) they locked eyes. Robin melted inside. "Should I run over to him? Should I ignore him?" Although she was unsure what to do, Josh casually walked up to her and said, "Hi." She blushed and stammered. Her heart skipped a beat. By the time they parted, she was sure she would love him forever.

Robin couldn't wait to tell Lisa about what happened. No sooner was Josh out of sight than she was dialing her best friend on her cell phone, chattering away about every detail of the Event.

Over the next several days Robin could hardly concentrate on school work.

"I wonder what it would be like to hang out with him."

"What would the other girls think if they saw him with me?"

"I wonder what it would be like to go out on a date with him."

"What would it be like to kiss him?"

Then a few days later the phone rang...it was Josh. Somehow Robin held herself together enough to talk with him. Then the Question: "Would you like to go to a movie Friday night?"

Later she discovered, to her horror, that Lisa had told Josh that Robin "liked him." This is what had spurred his phone call. At first Robin was furious, but that quickly subsided as the thrill of the impending date set in.

As the pair went out to his car after the movie, Josh leaned over and kissed her. Robin melted in his arms. Within a week she had given him her heart and her virginity. Such is often the outcome of romantic fantasy.

It's easy to see how allowing oneself to give over to a perpetual Cinderella fantasy could lead to other problems. Brook Wayne is a young mother who teaches teenage girls the importance of guarding their affections and their hearts. She writes:

> Nearly every young woman has an intoxicating dream of being swept off her feet by Prince Charming. Hopes of romance can be so strong that she may spend hours fantasizing. These daydreams seem harmless enough, but sadly they can tear down a young woman's resolve to remain emotionally pure.
>
> Emotional purity is reserving your affections by refusing to give your heart and thoughts over to someone to whom you are not married (or committed to marry). It is consecrating each aspect of your life before the Lord. (II Corinthians 10:5) Young men and women should view each other as brothers and sisters in the Lord with all purity, rather than romantic pursuits. (I Timothy 5:2)
>
> Some parents excuse their daughter's romantic fantasies by saying, "It is natural and common for young women to be dreaming and thinking about young men." Certainly it is common and natural for the flesh, but this does not make it right, nor does it prove that purity of the mind is unattainable.
>
> Love is beautiful in a God-ordained, covenant relationship. Yet, outside of that context, romance can have painful consequences. As desires are fed and encouraged, the longing to indulge them will intensify. Does any good *really* come from mentally wandering

in romantic visions? Eventually, the desires of the mind *will* result in external expression: dressing to catch the eyes of young men instead of behaving modestly, and sneaking around the authority and protection of parents...
    Who often buys romance novels? Married women! Having been discontent while single, satisfaction in marriage becomes elusive. To avoid this pitfall, women should abstain from novels and movies that promote unscriptural relationships. Instead they should turn their hearts to their family and invest themselves in the things of the Lord. Evaluate every thought, magazine, conversation, and TV show.[1]

Of course, it goes without saying that romantic fantasizing and the desire to be emotionally bound with a man is not limited to teenagers. Most women carry this unspoken mindset into their adult years.

A classic example of what many women experience in life is, believe it or not, Christian speaker and authoress Kay Arthur. Before she became truly converted to Christ, she too was driven to find a man's love. "Until I was twenty-nine," she writes, "I longed to be held in the arms of a man. I wanted security, and I thought that it was to be found in a man who would draw me to himself, lay my head on his chest and become my protector, my sustainer for life. This ideal was the epitome of life. It was all I wanted."[2]

She thought she found this in Tom, her first husband. As it turned out, he didn't have the emotional strength she was searching for and the marriage ended in divorce. Her bitter experience with love did not diminish her sanguine hopes. "I began my search," she continues. "I went from one man to another. In the process, I became something I never wanted, never dreamed I would ever be. I became an adulteress. Yet all I wanted was security."[3]

Addicted to an Emotional High

Gloria also became very promiscuous, but the deeper issue was her desire to be emotionally attached to men. What began in middle school as a desire to "go steady," grew over the years into an insatiable passion to have men want her. "I was hooked on sex and emotional attachments," she says. "I couldn't separate the two. If I had sex, I became emotionally attached. If I became emotionally attached, I would give myself to the guy out of fear of losing him."

During her high school and college years, Gloria had a succession of sexual relationships. She was so needy for male affection that she felt lonely and unfulfilled if she wasn't receiving it. If she wasn't romantically involved with someone she felt as though there was a gaping hole inside her—as if she was not complete as a person.

The more she gave over to this lust for male affection, the more insane her thinking became. "This dependency made me rely more and more on myself to sustain the relationship. I would spend hours thinking of ways to manipulate my boyfriend into being dependent on me. Then if I wanted to break up with him, I would try to find a way into some other guy's life."

While she was obsessed with the emotional high she received from being in a relationship, just as real was her fear of being rejected. If the affair began to lose its passion, Gloria would always make sure that she was the one to break it off. The thought of being rejected was simply too painful. However, before she would make the break she would make sure to have another guy lined up.

During college, her thinking became completely preoccupied with men. "I remember having tremendous difficulty studying because I was so consumed with lust and fear," she says.

Having a man was no longer the fun, carefree experience it had been when she was younger. Her thinking became increasingly dominated by jealousy, envy and fear. Gloria was miserable. "I didn't want to be alone, but I felt all alone. I didn't feel loved. I felt like an object; a very used object. I actually felt sick to my stomach most of the time. I lost a lot of weight because my insecurity of being alone affected my appetite."

When the Husband's Failure Leads to Adultery

Many women set themselves up for misery and even sin by bringing unreal expectations into marriage. Instead of entering marriage with a down-to-earth perspective about the normal struggles two young people will inevitably face, many new brides have lived in a fairytale fantasy for so long that the problems they should have been expecting, instead, seem insurmountable.

Vicky's story is a tragic example of this. She was a 20-year-old virgin when she married Carl. "My husband put me on a pedestal at that time, and I felt like the most beautiful, loved and important person in the world," she recalls. Marriage was everything she had hoped it would be. She assumed the honeymoon would last the rest of their lives.

"We had a good marriage, seemingly no problems of great concern besides normal financial issues," she says. "I was committed to stay at home with the children, so he needed to find a well-paying job. He became a state corrections officer, and that is when the unraveling began."

In the state prison, Carl faced two unexpected devils: overwhelming stress and an abundance of pornographic magazines. The one drove him to the other. Vicky began finding magazines hidden around the house. Each time she would confront him he would hang his head in shame, apologize and vow never to do it again. But he did—time and again.

Things got even worse when they purchased a computer and went online. This opened up an entire realm of forbidden pleasure to the young prison guard. He became obsessed with adult websites. "If I left the house even for a moment he went straight to the computer, Vicky says. "If the kids were home, he would find a way to keep them busy so he could view his pornography."

After nine years of this addiction, Carl finally repented and got his life right with God. He left his job at the penitentiary and, to help make ends meet, Vicky got a job in a real estate office. Unfortunately, by this time, he had created an enormous problem in his marriage. Not only had she become deeply resentful toward him because of the pornography, but she felt that he had destroyed what she had expected to be a perfect marriage.

"Now I became the one struggling," she says. "The many times I had been hurt over the years snowballed on me. Bill, a guy at the office, was very, very nice to me. He made me feel like I could be up on that pedestal again. I felt pretty and enjoyed the thought that he may have a little crush on me. The love I had felt for my husband that was numbed and eaten away over the years, I now felt for him."

One day, Bill offered to take her to lunch and she agreed. A friendly tap on her arm sent a surge of excitement through her body. Their eyes became locked on each other. Their affair began in a nearby motel that day.

Vicky found out too late that being in the arms of another man would not bring her the happiness she had sought from her husband. Now *she* became the deceiver, the conniver. Now it was *her* heart that was eaten out by sin. Now *she* was the one who had to face the consequences of sin.

The Emotional Life of a Woman

The fact of the matter is that women tend to be far more emotional than men. For instance, when I (Kathy) decorate the house, I am consciously trying to create an atmosphere of comfort and peace. After I have done my utmost to put my creative genius into our "nest," such as cleverly decorating an end table, Steve will often come along later and shove aside all the "nonsense" so he can throw his keys and other assorted items on the table. Another source of light-hearted contention is our beautifully decorated dining area; its crowning decoration being the gorgeous bouquet of silk flowers adorning the table. Without fail, morning, noon and night we follow the same ritual. When it's time to eat, he impatiently moves the bouquet to some remote location (all the while wondering why this monstrosity has to be in the way!) and I go behind him after the meal and put it back. These are cute little quirks between us, but they perfectly illustrate one of the differences between men and women. Women tend to be emotional, while men tend to be practical and logical.

This carries over into sexuality, as well. Men are apt to be stimulated visually, while women tend to become stimulated through their emotions. A man can have absolutely no feelings whatsoever for a woman and still completely enjoy having sex with her. I can remember so well the conversation Steve and I had when it came out that he had been unfaithful to me. I felt devastated because to me—he was giving his heart to another woman. Although he told me he felt nothing for the woman (who was typically a prostitute), it was very difficult for me to believe it. I always attached my feelings to sex and could not fathom that anybody could have sex without feelings. Later, I would come to understand that men have this capacity.

Women almost always attach emotions to their sexual activity. Very few women can become intimate with a man without some kind of emotional bond being in place. It has been said that men give love to receive sex in return, while women give sex to receive love in return.

As we have already seen, the danger for women is that their perceived need for affection can lead them down dangerous paths. In her book, *Lies Women Believe and the Truth that Sets*

Them Free, Nancy Leigh DeMoss, touches upon two issues that are very relevant to our subject matter. Lie #32 in her book is, "If I feel something, it must be true." She writes the following about it:

> The Enemy wants us to believe that if we feel unloved, we are unloved. If we feel we can't cope with the pressure, it must be true that we can't make it...
>
> The Truth is that, due to our fallen condition, our feelings often have very little to do with reality. In many instances, feelings are simply not a reliable gauge of what is actually true. When we allow them to be tied to our circumstances—which are constantly changing—rather than to the unchangeable realities of God and His Truth, our emotions are prone to fluctuate wildly.[4]

Lie #33 is also very pertinent: "I can't control my emotions." In regard to this falsehood, she writes:

> The Enemy uses this lie to make us believe we have no choice but to be controlled by our emotions. While it may be true to some degree that we can't help the way we feel, the Truth is that we don't have to let our feelings run our lives...
>
> If we accept the lie that we can't control our emotions, we will also believe we can't control how we act when we are feeling emotionally vulnerable or out of control. Not only are we too quick to believe our feelings, we are also too quick to obey them...
>
> Certainly what happens in our bodies does affect us emotionally, mentally, and even spiritually. We cannot isolate these various dimensions of who we are—they are inseparably intertwined. But we fall into the trap of the Enemy when we justify fleshly, sinful attitudes and

responses based on our physical condition or hormonal changes.[5]

While it is true that women are much more prone to make decisions based upon emotions, they don't have to be controlled by them. Throughout this book we will discuss how a Christian woman can break free from what can be a powerful "need" for a man's affection through the experience of repentance and maintaining a life in the Spirit.

CHAPTER THREE:
WORSHIP ME

*"All these things I will give You,
if You fall down and worship me." (Matthew 4:9)*

Brittany is determined to have breast enhancement surgery. She feels that it will significantly improve her looks. Her mother, who has had her own cosmetic surgery, says that if it will make her feel good about her body then she should do it. Brittany is 12-years-old.

Betty is a 45-year-old fitness buff. She pushes herself in the gym and goes on long runs three times a week. What little she eats usually only consists of fruits and vegetables. Most people consider her to be a "health nut," but the truth is that she is terrified of growing old and losing her figure.

Lois is now 55-years-old with a long history of cosmetic surgery. When she was still in her 30's she received breast implants. While in her early 40's she received a face lift. Not long after this she went through the excruciating ordeal of lip-enhancement surgery. Later she received a "tummy tuck" and a "butt lift." Lois looks in the mirror admiringly, not realizing that, to others, her face has a plastic, slightly deformed look.

These stories reveal a trend among women that is growing at a disturbing rate. Women are becoming increasingly concerned about their looks. Consider the growth of this industry. From

2000 to 2005, Botox treatments increased 388%, while the number of butt-lifts grew 283%.[1] In 2005, the top five cosmetic surgery procedures were liposuction (324,000), nose reshaping (298,000), breast augmentation (291,000), eyelid surgery (231,000) and tummy tucks (135,000).[2]

Mature women aren't the only ones participating in this growing movement. According to Dr. Phil, "more than a quarter of a million kids had plastic surgery" in 2006.[3]

It would be a mistake to dismiss all of this as nothing more than a passing fad. The truth is that prosperity and technological advances have simply made possible what women have always desired: the ability to make themselves look more beautiful.

While nobody would argue that it is simply a normal part of being a woman to want to be attractive, this growing self-absorption is cause for alarm.

Contributing Factors

The fact is that we are all, to one extent or another, a product of our culture. And in the American culture, women who are the smartest, the most capable, and yes, the most beautiful are the ones who are most richly rewarded. Girls learn early on that the primary source of their value as a human being comes by way of their looks and even their sexual desirability.

Teen icons such as Britney Spears and Christina Aguilera teach young girls to think sensually, dress seductively and act provocatively. Fashion designers market sexy lines of clothing with risqué ads. One of these, Abercrombie & Fitch, was recently criticized for its line of thong underwear for little girls and a pornographic catalog distributed to kids.

Television producers have also jumped on the band wagon. Trendy shows such as *Friends, The OC, One Tree Hill*, and many others, are teaching girls to associate free, unrestrained sexual expression with success, happiness, power and "love." The average American adolescent will view nearly 14,000 sexual references per year on TV.[4]

Then there are the magazines, such as *CosmoGIRL*, which are aimed directly at adolescent and teenaged girls. They too are promoting the mentality that a girl's self-worth is found in her sexiness. Feature articles in such magazines focus on subjects like how to seduce the cutest guy in school, sex tips, etc.

And when the current crop of teen idols, clothing designers, TV shows and magazines become obsolete, they'll be replaced by others with new names which still promote the same skewed message about sexuality and love.

Without a doubt, this constant message is having its effects. Consider some of the following startling facts that have emerged from various surveys of young people:

- 61% of all high school seniors have had sexual intercourse and 21% have had four or more partners.[5]
- Approximately 20% of teenagers had engaged in sex before turning 15 years old.[6]
- There are 4 million cases of sexually transmitted diseases among teens annually.[7]
- Each year there are three-quarters of a million teen pregnancies.[8]
- Over half of teens aged 15-19 in a recent poll had engaged in oral sex.[9]
- According to one study, between 44% and 90% of children between the ages of 8 and 16 have visited an adults-only website.[10]

It seems that girls are learning to use sex as a means of gaining affection and attention at increasingly younger ages. Some of the latest fads to hit *junior* high schools are oral sex, lesbianism and orgies. Young girls are giving oral sex to multiple guys—sometimes at the same time. Others are engaging in bisexual experiences for the express purpose of putting on a show for their boyfriends. Group sex is becoming increasingly more popular among teens. Just to show how morally calloused many of these young girls are becoming, one practice currently in vogue is to wear color-coded wrist bands which let guys know how far they will go: a green bracelet might mean she will perform oral sex; a purple one could mean she will go all the way; blue stands for a willingness to be involved in an orgy. For many of these girls, the only enjoyment they derive from this illicit behavior is the attention they receive.[*]

It is commonly believed that most teenage girls become promiscuous simply because they want to win and keep the affection of a boyfriend. This is ostensibly the reason for their willingness to engage in sex, but there are deeper motivations at work within many of them which find their roots in childhood.

When a child doesn't feel as though she's receiving the love and acceptance she needs, a sense of inferiority begins to develop within her. This so-called "inferiority complex" is reinforced each time she experiences rejection or is emotionally hurt in some way. The child—who is only doing what comes naturally—gradually develops defense mechanisms to cope with being hurt in life. Unfortunately, these defense mechanisms are the embryos of pride that begin in childhood, are developed in the teen years, and are perfected in adulthood.

The more inferior the child is made to feel by the rejection of others, the more she will attempt to compensate for that lack of security by employing some outstanding feature to make herself look better than—or at least as good as—the other girls around her. It could be some particular talent. It might be her personality or even her intellectual ability. But for

---

[*] It should be noted that these activities are far more prevalent in high population areas which tend to be at the forefront of such fads.

a girl, the surest way to gain approval is through her looks.**

Put several hundred girls together for a school year and certain ones will emerge through this highly competitive environment to be the most admired—or at least the most envied. A number of factors come into play as to which girls actually become the most popular, but there is no question that the prettiest or most buxom girls have the greatest advantage.

Girls who use their beauty to push their way to the top do so at the expense of others. Unwilling to be considered average, they do everything within their power to elevate themselves over their female rivals. This deeply competitive nature is simply an ugly form of pride. The more aggressive a girl is to rise to the top, the more likely her ambition is fueled by a deep-seated insecurity. The level of her insecurity usually determines the strength of her pride. Like sin of any kind, pride creates a downward spiral of soul degradation. The more one gives over to pride, the more that pride demands. In other words, it strengthens itself.

There is another factor that must be considered as well: the devil. As the young girl grows and suffers the inevitable pains of childhood, undoubtedly the enemy is present to show her how to respond to this pain. *Pride is the devil's solution to emotional pain.* In a fallen, sin-cursed world in which pride is exalted, this ungodly attitude is carefully cultivated as the young girl grows into adulthood.[11]

Pretty girls learn early on that their looks will gain them admiration from others, the attention of guys, and respect from everyone. Girls can be ruthlessly competitive with each other. Indeed, sometimes beautiful girls are the ugliest people around.

The fact of the matter is that beauty equates with power. The more desirable a woman is, the more she will tend to get

---

** Many girls who have been raised in good homes give over to sexual sin in spite of the fact that they feel emotionally secure. They simply do it because they enjoy it.

her way. Girls learn early on to use their sexual desirability to their advantage.

Little wonder then that a young girl emerges from her teenaged years with the firmly entrenched mindset that she must do everything possible to enhance and accentuate her feminine charms. If she isn't naturally beautiful, she might attempt to gain attention in other ways.

This desire for male attention is one of the primary reasons women become involved in sexual activity that is, at the very least, displeasing to the Lord. Sometimes it simply means becoming promiscuous with one's boyfriend. Other times this motivation plays out differently.

Craving Attention

One of the ways a woman can quickly gain a man's attention is through flirting. Some women playfully tease men with no intention whatsoever of going to bed with them. They simply enjoy being noticed by them. Take Latisha, for instance. "I loved the feeling of power I had over a man when I teased him," she says. "I knew that he would do whatever he needed to do to get what he wanted, so I took as much as possible without giving in."

Other women are flirtatious for the express purpose of enticing men into bed. Beth was one such woman.

When she was a teenager, she would do nearly anything to gain the attention of guys she was interested in. Sometimes she would playfully hit them on the arm, rub their arm, wink at them or bump into them. She would also call them cute names, give them swooning looks with her eyes or present them with a flirtatious smile.

As she grew older she found new ways to be noticed by guys. "I learned how to come up close behind a boy so he could feel my nearness or lean close to him and talk softly in his ear," Beth remembers. She learned to flatter guys by complimenting them on their outstanding features. She would actually study a man to learn what his interests were and how best to flatter his ego. Soon it became a game to her to see if she could win a guy. She became very manipulative and knew what would snare them. Her success at enticing men caused her to become increasingly conceited.

Another method Beth employed to gain attention was to alter her walking style. If the young man was behind her, she learned to throw her hips in a seductive manner. If she was walking toward a good-looking guy, she walked in such a way as to create a bounce.

By this time she was looking to entice guys into bed. "If I became romantically interested, I became seductive and started to dress in a manner to attract the guy physically by wearing lower-cut blouses, shorter skirts, tighter pants, styling my hair in a sexy way and using perfume that would arouse his senses."

Beth also made comments that had sexual overtones in them to show that she was sexually interested: e.g. "I really like going skinny-dipping."

"I eventually became so obsessed with getting the attention of men that I would actually try to charm married men into thinking I was more wonderful than their wives. How sick is that?"

Dressed to Kill

Lisa also enjoyed being noticed by men. Rather than behaving flirtatiously, she would gain their attention by the way she dressed. She became so jaded in the way she flaunted her body that she would even wear "sexy" outfits to church.

This 25-year-old "Christian" girl never really thought through what she was doing, why she was doing it or where her actions were taking her. She was simply enjoying the attention.

Because she was so consumed with herself, she was oblivious to the fact that she was causing guys at church to stumble into sin. All she knew was that when she showed off her full figure by wearing low-cut blouses she was sure to draw the attention of the cutest guys.

Lisa considered herself to be a Christian. She didn't mind using her body to get men to stare at her, but she had no interest in having sex before marriage. In fact, she fully planned to marry a Christian man.

When a cute guy named Phil started attending her church, she was determined to capture his attention. She purposely wore her sexiest outfits around him. Sure enough, it wasn't long before the two of them were an "item." Within a year, they were married.

Lisa wanted a man who would worship her body and that is exactly what she got. What she didn't take into account was that Phil was drawn to her sexiness because he was secretly addicted to pornography. He wanted a Christian wife, but godliness was not high on his list of considerations. He had other things on his mind.

In her pride and self-deceit, Lisa had convinced herself that Phil worshiped her body. He did, for awhile. But it wasn't long before he grew bored with her and returned to the thousands of naked bodies he could view on the Internet.

Lisa was devastated when the truth came out. She eventually called Pure Life Ministries looking for help. "I had no idea!" she exclaimed incredulously. "He deceived me! I'm going to divorce him!" As we talked and the whole story came out, I (Kathy) was able to help her see her own backslidden condition.

"My dear, the reason you couldn't discern who you were really marrying was because you have been so far from God yourself. Can't you see that you wanted a man who would worship your body and that's exactly what you got? If you divorce Phil without changing your heart, you will simply attract the same type of man again. You have relied on your looks for your value as a person, but what will be left for you when age takes its toll on your body and you are no longer desirable?" Surely it is true: "Charm is deceitful and beauty is vain, *but* a woman who fears the Lord, she shall be praised." (Proverbs 31:30)

The Making of a Sex Goddess

The ultimate form of pursuing ego-fulfillment through the attention of men is found in the sex-for-sale industry. This entire realm—encompassing strippers, prostitutes and erotic movie actresses—is all built around the desirability of the female body.

While the prostitute makes money satisfying a man's lust, the porn actress and the striptease artist make a living by inflaming it. For instance, a stripper can make as much as $100,000 annually—most of which is never reported to the I.R.S.

The clearest example of a person receiving the worship of others is found in the strip club, where there are sometimes as many as 200 fervid men lusting over a girl who is standing over them doing a table dance.

Jodie had studied dance from the time she was a little girl. When she was 20-years-old, she ran into an old friend from school who was making a lot of money stripping. "I had always been intrigued with the whole idea of getting boys' attention," she says. "I thought, 'Hey, I can dance on a stage.' It was kind of difficult, at first, to get naked in front of a bunch of strangers, but as a young dancer with Madonna as my idol, I was like a fish in water. I finally felt in complete control of something. It was also about looking to please men and being what they wanted."

David Sherman spent 14 years running strip joints and became an expert at manipulating girls into stripping. He offered the following testimony about strippers before the Michigan House Committee on Ethics and Constitutional Law.

> [Strippers] get used to being objectified. It becomes as important to them to hear how beautiful they are 200 times a day as it is to actually make the money from the dancing.
>
> Between the use of drugs to medicate what they do and hearing how beautiful they are all the time, they soon experience what I call BDA—Basic Dancer Attitude. This is when the dancer thinks that no matter what friends, children, husband and families think about her, it doesn't matter. They can all be replaced because all of the patrons around her find her attractive, beautiful and idolized.[12]

The porn star doesn't perform before a group of leering men but in front of a cold camera. She is paid a lot of money to have sex with strangers—both male and female—in a closed setting where only a producer, director and stage crew is present.

By its nature, pornography is produced for the purpose of creating intense lust. Some of these girls gain huge followings of fans that idolize them. They have been the object of an incredible amount of sexual passion by these men. One former porn star wrote that she participated in the industry "…for the lust of power and the love of money."[13]

With the advent of the Internet, women are finding that they can produce their own pornography outside of the adult entertainment industry. Tammy, a girl in her early 20's, describes what she became involved in.

> While I was in college, I had been sexually involved with a guy from school. He moved away after he graduated and we continued the relationship

online. I posed for pictures, performed sexual acts on video for him, etc. That evolved into putting a show on the Internet for others every night from my bedroom. At the same time I became increasingly involved in viewing online pornography myself. I also became much more promiscuous. When I went into this, I had no idea how it would destroy almost every normal relationship I attempted to have.

Believe it or not, during this whole time I was an active leader in my church. Nobody there had any idea about this secret life. I wanted to reach out for help, but I was afraid of exposing what I was doing to the people at the church. I spent months hurting, feeling like even God couldn't help me anymore.

Prostitutes, who are also in the business primarily for the easy money, gain a different side benefit. Cindy, who became not only a prostitute but also a madam, ran an escort service. "To me, it was a huge adventure," she recalls. "The power trip was enormous. I could turn men down, decide what to do with whom, dress however I wanted, pick which girls would be with which men, and so on. I loved having that kind of control, but eventually I quit the business out of fear of getting busted."

Whatever the motivations are at work in a girl's heart to cause her to perform sexual acts for money, it isn't long before she begins paying a price she never expected. Shelly Lubben was once a prostitute, stripper and porn actress. She says that on their days off girls involved in the industry would "…walk around like zombies with a beer in one hand and a shot of whiskey in the other."[14]

Bob Harrington, who spent years ministering to the strippers in the French Quarter of New Orleans, describes the outcome of the girls who flock there with dreams of stardom.

Once they arrive on Bourbon Street, the competition among them is ferocious—fresh, beautiful young bodies vying for the opportunity to take their clothes off in front of sex-hungry men...

Some consider stripping a springboard to a Hollywood contract and fame. They know that Marilyn Monroe made it big after she posed in the nude for a calendar...

But what none of these girls realize is that Bourbon Street is the end, not the beginning, of the road. They soon fall prey to the corruption of the atmosphere—hustling customers for drinks, prostitution, drug addiction, lesbianism, posing for pornographic photographs and performing unspeakable acts of perversion in stag movies.[15]

The End of This Road

There are few sadder pictures than the woman who has lived her entire life for the attention of men, only to helplessly watch as her body succumbs to the ravages of time. In one sense, this is just as true of the average woman as it is of a sex worker. The following is part of an email that came to us from a lady whose value system speaks for itself:

I have been a widow for 5 years now after a marriage of 25 years. I am a very physical and passionate woman. I love sex. I remained celibate and waiting on the Lord for 4 years of my widowhood, but in the last 6 months after losing 40 lbs. and some surgical help, I have been attracting men 10, 15, and 20 years my junior who think I am close to their age! I have given in to my passions but am consumed by guilt and fear of judgment!

This is a woman who is at least in her fifties and yet is still consumed with a lust to be sexually desirable. Even if she undergoes every cosmetic surgery treatment available, how much time will it really buy her? One can see this same pitiable attitude played out regularly in the retirement havens of Florida, where some elderly ladies stroll the beaches with skimpy bathing suits that seem to beckon for men's attention. It is clear that they have spent their whole lives in the pursuit of the unsatisfying ego fulfillment that comes from gaining the attention of men.

The Apostles Paul and Peter could have been writing to these women when each addressed the subject of female modesty. Let's take a moment to look at both of these passages. Paul wrote: "And I want women to be modest in their appearance. They should wear decent and appropriate clothing and not draw attention to themselves by the way they fix their hair or by wearing gold or pearls or expensive clothes. For women who claim to be devoted to God should make themselves attractive by the good things they do." (I Timothy 2:9-10 NLT)

There are two things that stand out in this passage of Scripture. First, the way a woman dresses. Look at the words the Apostle uses: *modest, decent, appropriate.* One translation says that they should "be dressed in simple clothing, with a quiet and serious air." (BBE) Paul specifically says that women should not dress to "draw attention to themselves."

The other thing he mentions is that they "should make themselves attractive by the good things they do." The Amplified Bible characterizes these good things as "deeds in themselves good and for the good and advantage of those contacted by them." Paul is painting a picture here of a woman whose beauty is seen in her modesty and in her goodness—her character.

Likewise, Peter wrote: "Your beauty should not come from outward adornment, such as braided hair and the wearing of gold jewelry and fine clothes. Instead, it should be that of your inner self, the unfading beauty of a gentle and quiet spirit, which is of great worth in God's sight. For this is the way the holy women of the past who put their hope in God used to make themselves beautiful." (I Peter 3:3-5a NIV)

Man looks upon the outward, but God sees the heart. He realizes something that many women overlook: A woman's body ends up in the ground, but the inner self—who she really is—lives forever. No wonder it is so important to cultivate godliness! No wonder the godly inner life of a woman is said to be "of great worth in God's sight."

The word *unfading*, which is employed by the NIV, is a very interesting term. The Greek word is *aphthartos*. The prefix "a" in the Greek language is the same as the English prefix "un." It shows the opposite of something: *un*-godly, *un*-believer, etc. The remainder of the word is *phthora*. Peter used this word in his second epistle when he wrote, "For…you may become partakers of the divine nature, having escaped the corruption (*phthora*) that is in the world by lust." (II Peter 1:4) Paul used it similarly when he wrote, "For the one who sows to his own flesh will from the flesh reap corruption (*phthora*)." (Galatians 6:8) Thus, Peter is admonishing women to pursue beauty that is *incorruptible*.

When a woman lives to gratify her lower nature, it sets into motion a process of internal corruption. Her entire inner constitution—her heart, soul, mind, imagination, will—all of what comprises her personhood, begins to become warped into something misshapen. Sin has that effect inside a person.

But Peter is telling us that a godly woman has just the opposite process at work within her. She is becoming increasingly beautified inside. Earlier in his first epistle he wrote that God had made it possible for us "to *obtain* an inheritance *which is* imperishable (*aphthartos*) and undefiled and will not fade away, reserved in heaven for you." (I Peter 1:4) In short, this inner life in God will never decay but will live on forever.

By contrast is the inner putrefaction of women who spend

their lives obsessed with their outward appearance. What will they look like when there is nothing left but a soul?

C.S. Lewis vividly captured the eternal tragedy involved in such women in his masterpiece, *The Great Divorce*. The storyline of the book revolves around a group of people (ghosts) who are transported by bus from hell to the fringes of heaven. There they are met by heaven dwellers (Solid People) who attempt to convince them to let go of their respective idols so they can enter heaven. Every single person finds a reason he or she can't live without their particular object of obsession. The following story provides an apt conclusion for this chapter:

> I think the most pitiable was a female Ghost...This one seemed quite unaware of her [phantom-like] appearance. More than one of the Solid People tried to talk to her, and at first I was quite at a loss to understand her behaviour to them. She appeared to be contorting her all but invisible face and writhing her smoke like body in a quite meaningless fashion. At last I came to the conclusion—incredible as it seemed—that she supposed herself still capable of attracting them and was trying to do so. She was a thing that had become incapable of conceiving conversation save as a means to that end. If a corpse already liquid with decay had arisen from the coffin, smeared its gums with lipstick, and attempted a flirtation, the result could not have been more appalling. In the end she muttered, 'Stupid creatures,' and turned back to the bus.[16]

CHAPTER FOUR:
LUST, FANTASY AND MASTURBATION

*"For we also once were foolish ourselves, disobedient, deceived,
enslaved to various lusts and pleasures." (Titus 3:3)*

Amber began masturbating at the age of 7. "I didn't even know what it was then," she says. Soon after her 12th birthday she discovered a scrambled adult movie channel on television. Not long after this, she found her dad's stash of pornographic magazines. "By the age of 12, when I learned what I was doing, I was masturbating at least 3 times a day. This continued, and increased, well through college. Eventually, I discovered the Internet and all the fabulously FREE porn that was out there. I increasingly viewed it and masturbated daily from about 13-20 years of age."

In Carole's six years of marriage, she and her husband have only been intimate twelve times. It seems that Dave preferred viewing Internet pornography to making love to his wife.

The frustration she felt over his lack of attention has been the main reason that she began masturbating. "I have practically pleaded with my husband to be intimate with me. It has all fallen on deaf ears," Carole laments. "He says he has no desire for sex—it's too much work. This wouldn't bother me so much if he showed me love in other ways. But he just doesn't seem to care about me at all. There are times when the feelings are so overwhelming."

Resentment over the way her husband has treated her has played a part in Carole's growing masturbation habit. She knows it is wrong but has become so discouraged that she can't seem to muster up the determination to fight it.

Stacey and Jim's sex life was very similar. Jim's sex drive seemed to diminish over their 17 years of marriage. Finally, Stacey confronted him about his lack of attention and their situation improved somewhat. "One night I mentioned a fantasy I had about being with another man," she recalls. "I wasn't fantasizing about anyone in particular; it was just a vague scenario. Then he said that he had desires to be with other women. That conversation led us to begin watching pornography together."

Stacey didn't realize that she was opening the door for her husband to pursue his fantasies. Pretty soon he began visiting strip clubs. When they were being intimate, Jim would tell her about what goes on at strip clubs. This sexual talk heightened the arousal for both of them. "Eventually I needed to hear about it to come to a climax," she confesses. "I knew that it was wrong, but it was an addiction. Afterwards I always felt dirty, and even worse, I knew that my encouragement was dragging my husband into more sin."

Peggy's problems didn't begin until she was nearly 50-years-old. She too was frustrated, but her disenchantment came about as a result of a different problem: she had been happily married nearly thirty years and had never experienced an orgasm. During that time she had sought answers from doctors, counselors and books; she had even pleaded with God to "fix her." The problem persisted. This longstanding, nagging frustration contributed to what happened next.

My children were married and out on their own and my husband worked all night. I was alone. I was flipping through TV channels when I remembered someone telling me that a certain channel had X-rated movies on it. Curiously, I tried the channel. I only subscribed to basic cable so the channel came in very warped and wobbly. Still, I could make out scenes that shocked me by their raw content. I masturbated and that was the first time I achieved an orgasm in all my years of marriage. I think that is what motivated me to continue.

I would not subscribe to any adult cable channels but became frustrated by not being able to see more clearly on the wavy reception. My husband was very much into computers and had bought me one, but I did not spend much time on it. He happened to mention that I should be careful about pornographic pop-ups.

I questioned him about the possibility of porn being on the Internet and he told me that it was easy to access. Poor guy, he had no idea that he just planted a seed of destruction in me. And so, when he was gone at night, I would access the porn websites, drink wine to dull my conscience and spiral down into the muck. During the day I would cry to the Lord for help, but at night, I would shut the door to Him and dive into the dark. Sex with my husband improved slightly, but only in the physical sense and even then, there was much letdown. The desire for porn increased and became more perverted. I knew I was in trouble.

Each of these women faced a very real challenge to maintain a pure heart and life. From a human standpoint, one could certainly understand how each of them would indulge in fantasy, masturbation and even pornography. Nevertheless, we serve a holy God who commands His children to live holy lives as well.

The truth is that a woman will never have a pure heart as long as she vacillates about whether or not lust and masturbation are sinful. She must decide once and for all that both are wrong in God's eyes. If she is indecisive on this point, she will never have the courage to win the battle that lies before her. Her constant waffling will weaken any resolve to do the hard thing.

Likewise, the one who is looking for the path of least resistance in life will also lack the determination to fight for a pure life. Purity and godliness do not mean enough to her to warrant the effort. When convicted over her sinful thoughts and actions, she will find ways to excuse, blameshift or otherwise justify continuing to live in her sin.

On the other hand, the woman with a tender conscience is keenly aware of every infraction against the Lord. She recognizes sin for the ugly thing that it is. Immoral deeds, though seemingly insignificant to others, are viewed by her as monstrous crimes against a holy God. The woman with a soft heart also remains consistently open to the Holy Spirit's conviction. She is not looking to push the limits of sin—to see how much she can get away with—but to avoid it altogether. Sin, to her, is a poison which must be eradicated at any cost. This woman will be able to make the necessary commitment to find victory over sin.

The place to begin this journey into purity is to better understand the realm where this great struggle must take place.

Heart Issue

The first thing which must be understood is that Christianity begins and ends in the heart. That is true because every action a person takes can ultimately be traced back to the heart. It also explains why Satan puts such a premium on influencing, clouding, seducing and winning people's hearts.

The heart is primarily the realm of a person's emotions, feelings, affections, motives and attitudes. Just as the physical heart pumps life-giving blood throughout the entire physiological being, so too the inner heart of man functions as the nucleus of all that goes on in a person's life. It is the breeding ground for all one's thinking. Its Creator said, "For from within, out of the heart of men, proceed the evil thoughts." (Mark 7:21)

In many ways, a human functions like a computer. The human computer operates with the information that is stored in the "hard drive" of the heart. The heart could be called the *seat of influence* for a person's life; the seedbed where ideas are formed, attitudes developed and out of which thoughts spring forth. It is the essence of our being.

Another good way to illustrate this is to think of a person as a city and the heart as the seat of government. It is within this administrative center that public policy is formed and established. In turn, that policy permeates and directs the affairs of what goes on within that community.

The important position the heart occupies within a person can be seen in Scripture. We are told of a "tender heart" (II Kings 22:19), a "proud heart" (II Chronicles 26:16), an "unfeeling heart" (Psalm 17:10), a "broken and contrite heart" (Psalm 51:17), a "humbled heart" (II Chronicles 32:26), a "broken heart" (Psalm 34:18), a "wise and discerning heart" (I Kings 3:12), a "hard heart" (Ephesians 4:18), and a "clean heart." (Psalm 51:10) People are told to "rend" their hearts (Joel 2:12), seek God with all their hearts (Psalm 119:2, 10), and pour out their hearts before Him. (Psalm 62:8) We are told of those who deceive their own hearts (James 1:26), backslide in heart (Proverbs 14:14), spurn reproof in their hearts (Proverbs 5:12), and regard wickedness in their hearts. (Psalm 66:18) It's no wonder then that we are admonished to, "Keep thy heart with all diligence; for out of it are the issues of life." (Proverbs 4:23 KJV) Surely it is true: "the inward thought and the heart of a man are deep." (Psalm 64:6)

Defining Lust

There are a number of biblical terms which are used (in varying degrees) to portray sexual desire. The Greek word *epithumeo* is the one most often employed. Strong defines it: "to set the heart upon, that is, long for…"[1] Easton says it is, "sinful longing; the inward sin which leads to the falling away from God."[2] Another says it is "a longing for the unlawful, hence, concupiscence, desire, lust…the sensual desire connected with adultery, fornication."[3] While it really describes the fallen nature's longing for any kind of sin, it is most often associated with sexual immorality.

The temptation to lust can be separated into two primary categories. First, there is *reactive* lust. This occurs when a good looking guy—or girl—comes into view. The woman's response may range from a quick glance to a longing, sinful gaze.

What tends to be a greater issue with women is *proactive* lust. This occurs when the woman purposely uses the faculties of her mind for immoral purposes—with or without outside influence. This happens primarily through the imagination, one of the most fascinating and mysterious operations of the human mind. For instance, a woman can be sitting at home on the couch, but in her mind, she can transport herself anywhere.

For the woman given over to sexual sin, this imaginary life revolves almost exclusively around romance, and in her fantasy world everything always transpires just the way she imagines it. The guy in the fantasy is extremely attractive and always flawlessly charming. He is so captivated by her desirability that he goes wild over her. His only wish is to spend the rest of his life lavishing her with love.

The man's features can also be changed in an instant. One moment he is a muscular athlete. Perhaps later he becomes a mysterious European or a bronzed Latino. The variations are as numerous as the world's male population itself. Not only can the partner be changed instantly, so too, can the scenario. It may be the guy that she saw at the store that day "coming on to her." Later, it is her favorite television actor. Again, the possibilities are endless.

In the world of imagination, everything is perfect. She does not have to deal with rejection, these dreamboats all love her. He does not act rudely, nor is he looking to take advantage of her. His only desire is to spend the rest of his life serving her every emotional and romantic desire. What's more, the woman is safe in the realm of fantasy. She can throw herself into the most intoxicating situations without concern about venereal diseases, pregnancies or any of the other consequences involved in the actual act of fornication.

One of the problems with fantasy is that it can take very strange turns. When a woman is in the throes of passion, she becomes much more susceptible to thoughts that would typically repulse her. Take Debbie, for instance, who shares the following:

> Whenever my husband and I are making love, the only way I can become aroused, it seems, is if I start to fantasize. Then I try to block it out and it doesn't work. It may for a while, but it always comes back. The more aroused I get, the longer I hold on to the fantasy before I can block it from my mind. I finally give in to it and then I can usually climax.
>
> Most of the time my fantasies are about my ex-husband's father who was a pervert and was always trying to have his way with me. What I cannot understand is this: the thought of my father-in-law actually touching me makes me want to throw up. So why is it that I fantasize about something like this instead of the macho man at the filling station that normal women fantasize about?

Dealing with Lust

When Jesus began His ministry in Israel, He faced a wall of unbelief that had formed from years of cold formalism. The Sermon on the Mount was a fresh word from heaven to people who had lost the sense of reality about God. Theirs was a dead religion which stressed outward actions and de-emphasized what was going on inside the person. When addressing the important subject of morality, Jesus went right to the "heart" of the issue.*

> You have heard that it was said, "You shall not commit adultery;" but I say to you that everyone who looks at a woman with lust for her has already committed adultery with her in his heart. If your right eye makes you stumble, tear it out and throw it from you; for it is better for you to lose one of the parts of your body, than for your whole body to be thrown into hell. If your right hand makes you stumble, cut it off and throw it from you; for it is better for you to lose one of the parts of your body, than for your whole body to go into hell. (Matthew 5:27-30)

Before we just skip over these well-known (and to many, worn out) words, we should stop to examine an important term Jesus used in this passage which the NASB translates as stumble (Gk. *skandalizo*). It seems as though Jesus is saying, "If you occasionally have a spiritual lapse, you must sever the cause of it lest you be sent to hell." How could that be the case? Would Jesus really send a person to hell because he or she "stumbles" in sin every now and then? Since these words don't seem to line up with current views on God's grace, most people tend to think

---

* When addressing sexual sin, the Bible nearly always presents it as a male problem. It should go without saying that the same principles are applicable when the genders are reversed.

that Jesus really didn't mean what He said. But we want to say that Jesus made no mistakes in His statements. He said exactly what He meant to say and it is very dangerous to put oneself in the position of explaining away His words.

One of the reasons these words aren't taken very seriously by many Christians today is that the English translation used here is very weak. The Greek term *skandalizo* is much more alarming than our English term stumble. Perhaps glancing at a couple of other verses where this Greek word is used will give us a better sense of what it really means:

"And in a similar way these are the ones on whom seed was sown on the rocky places, who, when they hear the word, immediately receive it with joy; and they have no firm root in themselves, but are only temporary; then, when affliction or persecution arises because of the word, immediately they fall away (*skandalizo*)." (Mark 4:16-17)

"And at that time many will fall away (*skandalizo*) and will deliver up one another and hate one another." (Matthew 24:10)

In the context of these two passages, we can see that this term refers to spiritual apostasy. But is that really what Jesus is talking about? Isn't this term also used in a less dramatic way? Yes, and that is precisely the point. The strength of Jesus' statement about lust and masturbation should be understood in direct correlation to each individual's situation.

For instance, if we are talking about a godly woman who "walks with the Lord," but then—in a moment of uncharacteristic weakness—succumbs to temptation and lusts or masturbates, but repents and gets back on track, that would rightly be termed *stumbling*. On the other hand, the word stumble would not be the appropriate term to use for the woman who regularly indulges in lust or masturbation. Her sin is causing her to *fall away* from the living God.

Many professing Christians we have dealt with over the years have deceived themselves about their sin. They like to say that they "struggle" with lust or masturbation, when the truth is that there really isn't any struggle going on at all: they regularly give over to the passions of their flesh. Peter described people like this in the Church of his day: "They have eyes full of harlotry, insatiable for sin. They beguile and bait and lure away unstable souls. Their hearts are trained in covetousness (lust, greed)...Forsaking the straight road they have gone astray." (II Peter 2:14-15 AMP)

This is the sort of man or woman whom I believe Jesus is addressing in this passage: those who are habitually sinning. They don't occasionally slip into the gutter; they live there. It would be very foolish for such people to minimize the gravity of Jesus' words in this passage. Twice He declares plainly: "It is better for you to lose one of the parts of your body, than for your whole body to go into hell." Jesus only used the term hell on a handful of occasions; in this case he used it twice. The implication of His words is unmistakable and it would be exceedingly foolish to impose one's doctrinal system upon His statements in order to keep one's sin.

The deception many fall prey to is that since they remain faithful in their church attendance, they can't be considered as apostates. To them, a backslider is someone who has thrown off all semblances of Christianity and is living in open sin. However, much of the Bible is taken up with the hypocrisy of those who "honor [God] with their lips but their hearts are far from [Him]." (Isaiah 29:13)

The context of Jesus' statements in Matthew 5 revolves around the heart, the inward life. The point Jesus made is that even though a person may not be committing actual fornication, the very fact that their heart is full of lust makes them just as guilty as if they were actually practicing it. Thus, it is possible for an individual to be very far from God in his or her heart even though they still maintain an outward semblance of religion.

Masturbation

Throughout most of Church history, Christian leaders considered any form of extra-marital sexuality to be sinful. Masturbation was rarely discussed openly. When it was addressed, it was usually cloaked in terms like "self-abuse," or biblical words such as uncleanness (Gk. *akatharsia*) or lasciviousness (Gk. *aselgeia*). Only during the past 30 years, as psychology has gained ever-increasing credibility within the Church, has it been suggested that masturbation is acceptable behavior under certain circumstances.

Is the modern Church's progressively open-minded, liberal position regarding sexuality simply a relaxation of stodgy, unnecessary rules of conduct from the Victorian age? Or could it be that today's moral laxity is further proof of the Church's relatively backslidden condition? While occasions do exist wherein believers remain needlessly old-fashioned regarding particular issues, for the most part it seems that Christendom has become enormously contaminated by the sexualized culture in which we live, following one step behind an increasing wave of decadence. In our opinion, the acceptance of masturbation by some prominent church leaders is a vivid illustration of this.

Seemingly, most of these relaxed standards have entered Christianity through the psychological community. Please understand that psychotherapy, by its very nature, is based more upon human empathy than biblical mandate. A counselor can sympathize so much with a person's struggles that he or she loses sight of God's expectation for holy living among His people. This approach can solidify itself in the counselor's heart if the power of God isn't actively at work in his or her counseling. Lacking any hope that the person can really overcome these overwhelming temptations, the counselor's only answer is one of acquiescence: "The Lord understands that the habit of masturbation is too powerful to conquer. Therefore, it cannot be wrong."

Those with this mindset apparently overlook or minimize the truth of what Paul stated: "No temptation has overtaken you but such as is common to man; and God is faithful, who will not allow you to be tempted beyond what you are able, but with the temptation will provide the way of escape also, so that you will be able to endure it." (I Corinthians 10:13) A counselor or teacher who condones a habit simply because it seems too strong to overcome demonstrates a lack of understanding and experience of God's power to set the captive free.

Be that as it may, there are a number of reasons why we believe masturbation is wrong for the believer. First and foremost, God created sex as a means for a married couple to physically express their love to one another. It is a very special act, providing the closest possible intimacy two people can enjoy together. Marital sex affords the opportunity for a husband and wife to unselfishly provide mutual pleasure, and, of course, is also the practical means for a couple to have children. Underlying all of this is the lifelong commitment and deep devotion that only a married couple can share. This is God's idea of sexuality.

Our modern, pleasure-driven culture holds an entirely different mindset toward sex. Those who purpose to fill their lives with the temporal gratifications of this world view sex as simply one room in the vast pleasure palace of life. Masturbation is considered a person's right—as are nearly all the various forms of pleasure available in our day and age. The difference between the mentality of God's kingdom and that of the world can best be summarized by the words of Jesus: "If anyone wishes to come after Me, he must deny himself...For whoever wishes to save his life will lose it, but whoever loses his life for My sake, he is the one who will save it." (Luke 9:23-24) This is a perspective that worldly Christians refuse to embrace.

Whatever else may be said about masturbation, it is by its very nature a completely self-centered act. On a routine basis, the woman isolates herself and enters into total self-indulgence. This kind of activity represents the very antithesis of the disciplined life Jesus expects from His followers, and its selfishness is utterly foreign to the Kingdom of God.

Furthermore, masturbation is driven by lust and fantasy. Sex is not meant to be a mechanical, physical activity comparable to relieving oneself in the bathroom. Inherently, it must involve another person—if not physically then mentally. To generate the sexual excitement necessary to bring oneself to orgasm requires that a woman focus her thoughts upon someone else—a pornographic picture, the mental image of someone she has seen, or some sexual or romantic fantasy.

Lust and masturbation are not only wrong in themselves, but, perhaps even worse they open the door to all kinds of deeper perversions. We cannot begin to count the people we have ministered to over the years who never imagined where their indulgence of lust and masturbation would lead them. Anyone who starts down this road can quickly find themselves veering out of control.

CHAPTER FIVE:
THE PROCESS OF SIN

*"And if you say in your heart, 'Why have these
things come on me?' because of the number of your
sins, your skirts have been uncovered and violent
punishment overtakes you."* (Jeremiah 13:22 BBE)

Those who become bound up in habitual sexual
sin—even if it is no more than masturbation and/or
pornography—are actually addicted to a complex chain
of actions. It all begins with temptation, moves into the person's
particular routine, peaks in the actual act itself and ends with
the lingering, inevitable consequences. Compelling the person
through this entire sequence of events is a driving lust. Thus,
the woman is not merely hooked on the act itself but on the
whole unfolding drama. The book of James reveals this process
from a spiritual perspective:

> Let no one say when he is tempted, "I am being
> tempted by God;" for God cannot be tempted by evil,
> and He Himself does not tempt anyone. But each one
> is tempted when he is carried away and enticed by
> his own lust. Then when lust has conceived, it gives
> birth to sin; and when sin is accomplished, it brings
> forth death. Do not be deceived, my beloved brethren.
> (James 1:13-16)

Temptation always precedes the process of sin. Typically, the woman is simply engaged in her normal activities of life— working, running errands, watching television, and so on—when the thought of sexual sin enters her mind. It is either placed in her mind by one of Satan's emissaries or simply appears as a longing of the flesh. Regardless, the mere existence of temptation itself does not constitute sin.

In Homer's *Odyssey*, one reads of the adventures of a Greek legend by the name of Ulysses. During one of his adventures he encounters the "sirens" whose seductive songs invoked stark madness that would eventually result in the death of any who heard them. As Ulysses' boat prepared to cross by the coast of the "sirens," he stopped up his men's ears with wax so they could not hear the deadly song, while he listened tied securely to the mast. Only the ropes could restrain the madness that came over him. This illustrates a person being tempted. As that captivating thought starts looming, often the only way to resist it is to be "tied securely to a mast."

Solomon said, "For the lips of an adulteress drip honey, and smoother than oil is her speech." (Proverbs 5:3) This phrase describes how the devil presents temptation. Honey represents promised fulfillment. The temptation seems irresistible because it is laced with the deception that the act of sin will bring about tremendous pleasure and satisfaction. The tantalizing thought is presented and all else is forgotten; the act of sexual sin looks absolutely intoxicating, and therefore irresistible.

The smooth oil represents the craftiness of the enemy. He knows when we are at our weakest moment. He does not mind waiting for days or even weeks if it means a greater defeat for the Christian. Paul twice speaks of the "the schemes of the devil." (Ephesians 6:11, II Corinthians 2:11) The demonic forces of hell have been carrying out their "guerrilla warfare" quite diligently for a long time. Fully camouflaged and extremely calculating, they launch the perfect illusion, timing each consecutive attack "to steal, and kill, and destroy" (John 10:10) God's property.

Once Satan has managed to get a fish hook in the woman, at his leisure, all he needs to do is to give a gentle tug on the line to get the woman going. It often comes in the form of remembering past pleasurable experiences. Frank Worthen comments:

> FLASHBACKS: Very few sexual encounters in the gay life-style could be considered great. Almost always, there is an element of wishing it could have been better. Often we'd feel used, short changed and degraded after such an encounter. Satan, however, has a way of throwing flashbacks of previous sexual experiences at us. In the memories he presents, all negative connotations are written out. We remember only the positive.
>
> He also tempts us through our natural tendency to make associations. We're all triggered by certain music, smells, sounds and visual images. These evoke distinct, vivid memories of past experiences.[1]

Ronald Jenson talks about the "triggers" that often lead a person into sin:

> A trigger is any event or emotion which evokes an inevitable response. Planning thinks about both the triggers and the usual result they bring in you. What are your triggers?...If you can identify the thing which leads up to your difficult time, you can prepare for and outmaneuver defeat and failure.[2]

I (Steve) found in my life that there were three circumstances that usually proved disastrous for me if they all happened at the same time. The first, of course, was the actual temptation. Again, demons used perfect timing to implant their thoughts. They usually did not bother to tempt me unless they could synchronize it with the other two needed elements: the physical build-up and opportunity.

The physical build-up I would experience, if I had not had sex in several days, greatly increased my desire to act out. As my hormones increased, I would become immensely sensitized to sexual stimuli. Lastly, I had to be given the opportunity. For me, this usually occurred when my wife was at work.

A woman's place of employment can often have a lot to do with whether or not she will be in a position to give over to sin. For instance, if she works in a store, and cannot leave her job, she is less likely to get into trouble during work hours.

On the other hand, those in positions that provide a lot of freedom of travel or access to a computer in a private setting will be much more vulnerable to temptation. Jane is a good example of the former. She was a representative for a cosmetics company and would travel to other cities to visit department stores which carried her products. Over time she began using these trips to strange cities as opportunities to engage in anonymous sex. I (Kathy) suggested that she needed to find a different job. Hearing this, she looked at me with an expression of utter shock and quickly responded, "I love my job. I make good money. This job is *perfect* for me!"

"I don't doubt that your job is perfect," I responded. "The enemy is quite adept at providing jobs that are perfect for his evil designs. Jane, if victory over sin doesn't mean any more to you than giving up a job, you might as well resign yourself to a lifestyle of failure. You will never change," I informed her. Unfortunately, to my knowledge, she is still making good money at her job and continues to engage in fornication. She preferred her job over getting the victory.

Jenny was another woman who faced a similar "fork in the road." Her job involved a lot of work on the computer. But in the private setting of her office, she had become terribly addicted to Internet pornography.

Jenny seemed sincere when she asked me how to get free from her porn addiction. However, she had the same disappointed look on her face as Jane did when I suggested that she give up her job. She made good money and didn't want to lose her position. The thought of parting with her career seemed unreasonable—even outlandish. "Jenny," I asked with all earnestness, "do you prefer being a well-paid sex addict to being a godly woman?" She wasn't going to acquiesce without a fight, but those words plagued her for days. She had to make a decision that had enormous consequences.

In the end, she decided that her walk with God meant more to her than her job. She was willing to forfeit something of huge importance for the sake of her spiritual life. Later, the Lord honored her sacrifice and provided her with a job in a completely different line of work. She didn't make as much money as previously, but she really did enjoy her new career. Most important, she was once again right with God. Her attitude is an example of what Jesus meant when He said, "And if your right eye makes you stumble, tear it out, and throw it from you...And if your right hand makes you stumble, cut it off, and throw it from you; for it is better for you that one of the parts of your body perish, than for your whole body to go into hell." (Matthew 5:29-30)

The Idol of Fantasy

The initial step into sin is allowing the thought of temptation to fester. It is extremely difficult to thwart the processes of thought once entertained. James said that a person is tempted "when he is carried away and enticed by his own lust..." This illustrates a woman's lust actually picking her up and carrying her to a place where she cannot defend herself and *then* enticing her. It is almost as if her carnal desires momentarily take control of her mind and carry her away to some dream world where she is then utterly defenseless. Once there, she is swallowed up in the evil imaginations of her own fallen heart.

This is not something that she *does not* want to do. On the contrary, it is exactly what she *does* want to do. The NIV translates it, "but each one is tempted when by his own evil desire he is dragged away and enticed." It is not only the object of the temptation that she covets, but the actual temptation itself! She *wants* to fill her mind with that tantalizing temptation. It is no wonder that she has such a difficult time exercising self-restraint. Just as a person savors every spoonful of delicious pudding, the woman relishes every thought of the ultimate romantic encounter. The longer she allows herself to fantasize, the more likely she will act it out. She is, in essence, erecting an idol of fantasy. The longer she entertains the fantasy the larger the idol grows. At this point she is being enticed.

These thoughts are difficult to control because the woman sees only the instant gratification. The fantasy of the impending experience overshadows past vows to discontinue such behavior. All that lies in sight is the pleasure of the anticipated act. She completely forgets about God and loved ones. Her past attempts to quit are now lost in the sea of forgetfulness. It appears that she just cannot help herself. As the lust builds in her mind, her behavior becomes reckless. Things she never imagined doing under normal circumstances now become "great expectations." She is starting to enter into a trance, becoming like the dog mesmerized by a piece of meat held just out of his reach. Her heart begins to race, her breathing becomes short, and her palms begin to sweat. She is actually becoming intoxicated with desire. Dietrich Bonhoeffer best describes this struggle:

> At this moment God is quite unreal to us, He loses all reality, and only desire for the creature is real; the only reality is the devil. Satan does not here fill us with hatred of God, but with forgetfulness of God. And now

his falsehood is added to this proof of strength. The lust thus aroused envelopes the mind and will of man in deepest darkness. The powers of clear discrimination and of decision are taken from us.[3]

Physically Moving Toward Sin

The next step is taken when the body actually gets up and moves. The woman may fool herself into thinking she will just view some pornography and go no further, but she almost always does.

I (Steve) can remember thinking in my own mind, "I'll just drive by where the hookers are, just to see what they look like." Another way I would be deceived was by telling myself that I would only look at a magazine. The problem was, once I saw the magazine, I would enter into that mind-altered state where everything becomes sexual and nothing is forbidden. After looking through the magazines, I wanted to see the movies. As soon as I began watching the movies, I wanted the real thing.

A woman viewing pornography becomes warped in her decision making. Sin is never satisfied. One sin leads to another sin. One bad decision leads to another bad decision. Perhaps this is why the prophet Micah warned, "Woe to those who scheme iniquity, who work out evil on their beds! When morning comes, they do it, for it is in the power of their hands." (Micah 2:1)

The Point of No Return

Once the body is in motion, rationalization takes over. "Oh well, it's too late to stop now. I might as well get it over with!" This is "the point of no return." Now uninhibited and oblivious to all fear, guilt or the possibility of danger, the woman is fully convinced that this is the only reasonable route she can take. Solomon would describe her as a woman with, "An heart that deviseth wicked imaginations, feet that be swift in running to mischief." (Proverbs 6:18 KJV) Thus, the woman becomes totally committed to acting out her fantasy. The tidal waves of lust will carry her far out into the ocean of perversion where she so longs to be. Although she had intended only to check out her particular source of temptation, once she experienced the sights and sounds associated with her particular sin, the pull of sin overwhelmed her.

The Various Routines

Now different behaviors come into play. Each addict has her own fantasy—her own routine. Actually, this is where they find the real excitement. Note: The addict's routine begins immediately when she moves toward her sin. Just as the woman who is addicted to shopping thinks fondly of her favorite boutiques, the sales they are advertising, the excitement of a day out with the girls at the mall, and the all the new outfits she might enjoy wearing, the female sex addict thinks of the many things that comprise her routine. The actual routine varies with different people. Even the girl who only struggles with a habit of masturbation has a predictable pattern of behavior that makes up her sin.

I (Steve) personally spent nearly 15 years of my life during the 70's and early 80's obsessed with sex. In those days one had to go to an adult bookstore to see hardcore pornography. My routine usually began by browsing the magazine racks for awhile. As my lust heightened, I would venture into the movie arcade, a dimly lit area located in the rear of the bookstore containing a number of booths where a man could watch a pornographic film in private. I would "size up" the movie advertisements for each one, determining which one most appealed to me. Then I would go from booth to booth, saving my favorite for last. Other times I would view pornography as a precursor to visiting a prostitute or going to a strip club.

These days, people are more likely to do their cruising online. This is what Brittany would do. She had become addicted to Internet porn when she discovered it on her brother's computer. Before long she was searching it out on her own computer.

She really wasn't attracted to the guys; it was the bodies of other girls that turned her on. Her routine would actually begin earlier in the day when she would either remember some picture she had seen previously or just start thinking about the updates that would be posted on her favorite websites. Throughout the day the expectation about what she might see would keep her in a state of semi-excitement. After everybody went to bed that night, she would go online in the privacy of her bedroom. She was amazed at how the hours would race by, while she visited one explicit website after another.

But not everyone is satisfied with simply looking at dirty pictures. Their addiction has taken them much further than they ever imagined they would go. Whatever the particular form of sexual sin a woman may become addicted to, it is certain that a specific routine will play a part in the event.

Jane's routine always took the same basic form. She would typically catch an early flight to the city she would visit that week to sell her cosmetics. On the plane she would close her eyes and remember past experiences. Once she arrived, she would rent a car, put her things in her hotel room and make her rounds of the department stores. After grabbing a bite to eat and freshening up, she would head out in search of an upscale bar. Through all of this her anticipation would grow.

Once she arrived at the bar, she would scan the room for a guy who appealed to her. Having set her sights on some guy, she would be sure to make eye contact. After making her interest fairly clear, the man would eventually wander over and strike up a conversation. Before long, the two of them would be talking, laughing and having a good time together. A couple of hours and a few drinks later, she would invite him to her room.

To say that Jane was only addicted to the sexual act would be an oversimplification. She was hooked on the entire experience: flirting with the guy, teasing him, driving to the hotel with him in pursuit and even going up the elevator alone together. The sexual act would simply be the culmination of the entire experience.

Whatever form a woman's addiction might take, there will be a distinct or observable pattern which plays a major part in her "acting out" sexually. While the routines they give over to are different, each woman shares one thing in common: lust has been conceived in the heart, and each one is now on a personal mission to satisfy herself to the best of her ability.

The Act of Sin

Sin. The actual act. It is often a terrible disappointment after a prolonged period during which the fulfillment of the fantasy was anticipated. Nevertheless, it is the object of desire on which the woman has fixed her mind. Once she has entered into the trance and begun the routine, it is highly unlikely that she can stop herself from following through with some kind of sexual act. Once she has invested her time and energy into her fantasy, it will require something special to culminate the entire process.

Death

Finally, when the act of sin has been committed, it brings forth death: death of self-respect and death of feelings. It will also bring despair, anger, helplessness, hopelessness, guilt, condemnation, and vows never to do it again. It is a horrible price that Satan and his demons exact upon those deceived. First, they lead the woman by the nose into sin; then once committed, they condemn and attack her for being weak and despicable. The shame grows deeper and deeper.

Once the sexual act is over and the lust has drained from her body, she can begin to see the sin more clearly for what it is. The empty promises of the fantasy are nowhere to be found; all that remains is the horrible penalty for her sin. During the temptation she was oblivious to the consequences of her choices. Now, they are in full view. As Solomon laid out the presentation of sin, he described in riveting detail the consequences of giving in to sexual temptation. He brings it all to life in the following passage:

> For the lips of an adulteress drip honey, and smoother than oil is her speech; but in the end she is bitter as wormwood, sharp as a two-edged sword. Her feet go down to death, her steps lay hold of Sheol… Now then, my sons, listen to me, and do not depart from the words of my mouth. Keep your way far from her, and do not go near the door of her house, lest you give your vigor to others, and your years to the cruel one; lest strangers be filled with your strength, and your hard-earned goods go to the house of an alien; and you groan at your latter end, when your flesh and your body are consumed; and you say, "How I have hated instruction! And my heart spurned reproof! And I have not listened to the voice of my teachers, nor inclined my ear to my instructors!" (Proverbs 5:3-13)

On two different occasions, Solomon used the Hebrew word *aharit*. In verse four he says "in the end…" In verse eleven it is expressed "at your latter end." *Aharit* is the same word used in Proverbs 14:12: "There is a way which seems right to a man, but its end is the way of death." What Solomon has shown, is that the sin does not just disappear once it has been indulged.

The woman may have to face the results of her actions for a long time.

We have already mentioned the death that is experienced following each act of sin. In addition to these, there are also the long-term consequences of a lifetime of giving over to sexual sin. Adam Clarke comments on this passage:

> The mourning here spoken of is of the most excessive kind: the word *naham* is often applied to the growling of a lion, and the hoarse incessant murmuring of the sea. In the line of my duty, I have been often called to attend the death-bed of such persons, where groans and shrieks were incessant through the ejaculating pains in their bones and flesh. Whoever has witnessed a closing scene like this will at once perceive with what force and propriety the wise man speaks. And "how have I hated instruction, and despised the voice of my teachers!" is the unavailing cry in that terrific time. Reader, whosoever thou art, lay these things to heart.[4]

Resolutions and Repentance

As the woman enters the beginning stage of remorse, she will often make certain promises to God vowing never to repeat the same sin again: "Lord, I swear I won't do this ever again!" As her eyes are opened to the reality of the horrible emptiness and nature of her sin, she readily makes such a vow; for, it is at this moment that she truly sees sin for what it really is.

However, the problem with making such a resolution is that it stems from her own strength and determination to resist and overcome an evil. This sort of "promise-keeping" will never endure future temptations in the same area. It is for this exact reason that she has attempted countless times before to break the habit, yet to no avail.

The woman desperately needs repentance. True repentance comes when a person's heart has changed its outlook on sin. A woman will only quit her sinful, destructive behavior when she has truly repented of it in her heart. As she moves closer to the heart of God, she begins to develop a "godly sorrow" over her sin.

Overcoming Temptation

As the woman grows stronger in her Christian walk and closer to God, she begins to see the whole act of sin, including the consequences, rather than just the reward. Rather than concentrating on the delicious experience, she will be able to realistically see that past experiences usually were only mediocre, at best. Instead of focusing her thoughts on how much fun it might be, she will clearly see the consequences that await her: the *aharit*. She will recall the guilt-ridden days of shame, disgust, and condemnation. Worst of all, she will remember the feeling of being isolated from the Lord.

A woman will overcome temptation by refusing to dwell on sexual thoughts. When a fantasy enters her mind, she will make the conscious decision not to entertain it. The woman who affords herself the luxury of savoring a fantasy is setting herself up for a huge fall. The time to deal with temptation is when it *first* appears. The longer the thought lingers, the more difficult it is to resist.

A Way of Escape

One important aspect of dealing with temptation is that there is *always* a way out. Paul said, "No temptation has overtaken you but such as is common to man; and God is faithful, who will not allow you to be tempted beyond what you are able, but with the temptation will provide the way of escape also, that you may be able to endure it." (I Corinthians 10:13)

Paul said that God would "not allow you to be tempted beyond what you are able…" An illustration of the word "able" is the line that is drawn on the side of a ship. As the ship is loaded with cargo and sinks into the water, it approaches the point at which the "Plimsoll line" parallels the water level, indicating that the ship has been loaded to capacity. When the loaded ship sinks to where that line is under water, they know the ship has been overloaded. We are never tempted beyond our "Plimsoll line." We are never loaded with more temptation or testing than we can bear. God never allows our temptations to go beyond that line. He always provides for us a way of escape!

Thus, we must learn how to be sensitive to the escape route He provides. We can only learn His methods by studying His ways. This is the reason it is so important that we know where to go to find help. If we haphazardly seek out just any source for answers, we will likely be misguided and led further astray.

CREATE IN ME A PURE HEART

Part 2: THE RIGHT COURSE

CHAPTER SIX:
THE ROOT ISSUES

*"We have rebelled against you, rejected you,
and refused to follow you. We have... turned away
from you." (Isaiah 59:13 GNB)*

"Sex has always been a part of my life," Brittany states matter-of-factly. "It was one of the first things I knew about." It began when she was three years old and was fondled by a babysitter. Two years later, a 13-year-old cousin raped her and continued abusing her for three years. A couple of years after that ended she moved in with her grandparents, which put her within reach of some other cousins who molested her repeatedly over the years.

At one point, she decided to tell her parents about what had happened to her. "Well, if anything did happen it was your fault," her mother flatly told her. Her father simply said, "You should have told me; but boys will be boys."

Little wonder that Brittany became promiscuous at a very early age. Even after getting married, she regularly viewed Internet pornography in secret and occasionally had affairs. She was out of control but didn't know what to do about it.

In the spring of 2003, God brought an older woman into her life. "I call her Mom because in my heart she is my mom. She has loved me unconditionally. I shared with her my past, yet she saw the sin that was still there. She told me that I had a spirit of lust all around me and that I reeked with self-pity; she was so right."

Having a godly woman in her life was a big help, but her struggles continued. One day, Brittany called an old boyfriend and the two had sex in the back of her SUV. "I immediately felt guilty, but six months later we met again. I told Mom about both of these occasions."

The older woman told her that she was a sexual addict and needed help. She called her pastor who gave her the name of Pure Life Ministries. The two women each ordered a copy of *At the Altar of Sexual Idolatry* and went through it together. Brittany tells what has helped her find freedom.

> When I started this book well over a year ago, I was filled with lust and self-pity. It has been devastating to realize just how evil I have been. I would be lying if I said this has been easy; it has been the hardest thing I have ever done. The discipline has been the most difficult. I have always equated discipline with fear and hate, but I am learning that it is about love. I wish I could put into words what it is like to feel as if you are the greatest fraud and failure on the planet, and yet to know that, in spite of it all, God still chooses to love you. I truly know now that the Lord does discipline those He loves.
>
> There have been two things which have helped me most of all. The first has been the accountability I have received from Mom. She has loved me enough to confront me and keep confronting me. She has always encouraged me to go to God with my problems.
>
> The second thing has been the truth about myself and my problems that I have learned from *At the Altar of Sexual Idolatry*. There have been parts that did not pertain to me as a woman, so I skipped those; but 99% has been right on!

How am I doing now? I am crying as I write this because I never thought this time would come. Satan still tempts me on occasion, but I call on my Father first, then I call my Mom until the thought passes. I don't think I am totally free, but I am closer than I have ever been. God is doing things in my heart that I cannot describe; there are feelings I never felt before. I am not one to cry easily, but something about the Lord touches my heart almost everyday and I just weep…because I love Him and I know He's setting me free.

How many other women like Brittany are carrying around the pain and baggage of childhood abuse? Perhaps you, the reader, can relate to her story. The following statistics offer a glimpse into the scope of the problem in the U.S.

- One in six (16.6%) women have been victims of sexual assault.[1]
- The years 2004-2005, averaged 200,780 victims of rape, attempted rape or sexual assault.[2]
- About 44% of rape victims are under age 18, and 80% are under age 30.[3]
- 20% of underage girls will be sexually exploited.[4]
- The median age of victimization for females is 9.6 years.[5]
- Only 1-10% of child molestations are ever reported.[6]
- There are an estimated 60 million survivors of childhood sexual abuse.[7]

One of the most painful and traumatic things a young girl can experience is sexual molestation. Unquestionably, many women involved in sexual sin have been started down that path through childhood abuse. Our website survey revealed that approximately 33% of the struggling women who participated had been molested as a child—about double the national rate mentioned above. And when you think about it, it would stand to reason that a third of all women in habitual sexual sin have initially been influenced by sexual abuse.*

Pam is another young woman who suffered terribly as a child. She had been raised by an abusive stepfather who began molesting her at a young age. He even allowed some of his friends to have sex with her. As a teenager she rebelled and began having sex with practically anybody who wanted her. She continued with this reckless behavior even after becoming a Christian.

It was in the late 1980's, when we were still in California, that Pam came to Pure Life Ministries looking for help. She had been trying to find freedom for over a year but didn't seem to be making any progress. As we talked with her, one of the reasons became clear. She had been holding on to deep bitterness toward her stepfather.

Prior to coming to us she had been involved in counseling with a psychotherapist who minimized her present sin because of her past sufferings. The counselor saw her as a victim who needed to accept God's love, not as a sinner who needed to repent. Unlike "Mom" mentioned in Brittany's story, the therapist constantly reinforced the idea that Pam was not responsible for her present actions.

As difficult as it can be, sometimes we must confront a woman's sin head-on for her own benefit. Humanistic mercy says that we should treat Pam as a victim. God's mercy says that she is responsible for her actions as an adult, and unless she

---

* It should be noted that sexual molestation isn't the only form of victimization that can lead a girl into promiscuity. For example, others, who were not sexually abused, may have become promiscuous as a means of trying to overcome the rejection they experienced from unloving parents.

repents, she will remain separated from Him, stuck on a hopeless merry-go-round of sin, pain, and degradation. Misguided human sympathy only exacerbates the situation.

Pam later acknowledged that she had come to enjoy the attention and pity she received from her counselor. There was also a part of her (her flesh) that was happy to hear that she could keep her sin.

We told Pam that unless she was willing to let go of the past, forgive her stepfather for his crimes against her and begin to take responsibility for her present actions she would be destined to remain in habitual sin. Initially, she seemed stunned by what we told her. For years she had gained sympathy by recounting in detail the abuse she had suffered. Nobody had ever inferred that she was responsible for her present behavior. This revelation completely changed her perspective on life. From that moment on, she saw her sin as willful rebellion against God. She never again returned to her sin. She was free!

Dealing with the Present

The Bible clearly teaches the Christian woman who is struggling with sinful habits to deal with the *here and now*, instead of attempting to resolve problems by focusing on the past. There are numerous accounts in Scripture of men and women who suffered painful experiences—perhaps Joseph being sold into slavery by his brothers is the most notable example. But nowhere in the Bible do we find these individuals focusing on themselves, their suffering, or their past. What we see in Scripture is the account of these individuals looking to God to provide healing and meaning, as well as power to overcome their painful experience. We also see in Scripture the consistent application of forward-looking teachings, such as, repaying good for evil, forgiving as we have been forgiven, loving our enemies, denying self, giving to others in need, casting our burdens on the Lord, and meditating on the incomprehensible goodness and mercy of the sovereign Lord.

The Bible clearly teaches the struggling woman to deal with her sinful nature.** Can you imagine God saying, "You shall not murder…unless of course you were physically abused as a child, then it is understandable." How ridiculous! Yet, in the news, as well as on today's talk shows, many people make excuses and rationalize their mistakes and sinful lifestyles by pointing an accusing finger at their relatives or others from their past. The truth is, before a woman can ever hope to overcome habitual sin, she must first be willing to take responsibility for her *own* actions. This means dealing with one's present behavior without excuses. What has happened in the past cannot be changed. Consequently, those who are going to be victorious over sin must learn to forget what lies in the past and focus their attention on the present.

When David was confronted by the prophet Nathan over his affair with Bathsheba, his response was not to make excuses or blame others. In his heart-wrenching prayer of repentance, he pleaded with the Lord: "Cleanse me from my sin. For I know my transgressions, and my sin is ever before me. Against You, You only, I have sinned and done what is evil in Your sight, so that You are justified when You speak and blameless when You judge." (Psalm 51:2-4)

The first step toward victory over life-dominating habits is understanding that you are in your present circumstances because of the choices *you* have made for yourself. David took full responsibility when confronted about his sin with Bathsheba. He did not offer the pitiful excuses that can often be heard today: "I was going through a difficult period in my life." "It was the devil that set the whole thing up. God knows that I am a man with natural passions. What does He think a man would

---

** As we will soon discuss, Scripture clearly states that all humans have a fallen nature that is prone to sin. Nevertheless, the Bible is also unequivocal in its expectation that people turn from their sins.

do under such circumstances?" "My wife has been distant with me lately. No wonder I fell to the temptation!" David knew he was wrong. He made a conscious decision to do it—no one else. When God punished him for his sin, he did not blame God for somehow failing him. He humbled himself before the Lord and accepted the forthcoming punishment for his actions.

Blaming the Mate

While some blame their parents for their present problems, others blame their spouses. One of the justifications we have heard over the years goes something like this: "My husband has just not been there for me and when a man at work started paying attention to me, I went to bed with him." The woman who commits something as evil as adultery because her husband fails to pay enough attention to her is actually worse off in her heart than the adulteress who is simply out of control with her sex life.

In actuality, she is probably not being honest with herself. A sincere Christian would never consider adultery to be an option. She would be more inclined to examine her own life to determine whether or not the emotional expectations she is placing on her husband are too demanding. She would take her pain—as great as it may be—to the Lord in prayer. It is there, in the secret place with her God, that she will pour out her heart about how she feels neglected and unappreciated. Her petitions to the Lord to work in her husband's heart will not go unheeded.

Blaming God

As incredible as it may seem, many women try to blame God for their problems. Some actually get angry at Him because He "let them get this way," or because He will not immediately set them free upon their demand. It is not God's fault when people choose to walk in sin. He has graciously done everything He can to make salvation and liberty available to us. James says that God never tempts man. (James 1:13) Paul says let God be true and every man a liar. (Romans 3:4) Our beginnings may not seem fair, but we still cannot blame God. After all, He never makes any wrong decisions for us.

This is a very important step for some of you reading this book. Many of you will tend to skip over this section and disregard what is being considered here. But, we *must* take responsibility for our sin. We must tell God that we have sinned against Him and against others. This should not be done as some secret formula to receiving forgiveness, but with a heart-felt sorrow over the wrongfulness of our actions—godly sorrow leading to true repentance.

Blaming Emotional Problems

There is one more important subject we must touch upon here. Over the past 30 years, as the field of psychology has gained credibility and prominence in the Church, the idea has grown that people become addicted to various forms of sin as a direct result of emotional problems. The notion advanced is that mental disorders come about primarily because the person has unmet emotional needs (that are often supposed to be the direct result of failing to receive the proper emotional nurturing during childhood). Since the roots of the person's problems lie in the realm of emotions, the counselor must help the counselee understand and deal with those issues before she will find freedom from her addiction. The counselee is then typically led into months, or even years, of focusing on the great quagmire of emotions that fluctuate within, without experiencing any significant change in her behavior.

There are several brief points we must make regarding this line of thinking. First, it needs to be stated that for 2,000 years God has been successfully and powerfully transforming hopeless sinners into bright, joyful saints without the aid of psychology!

Second, it is an indisputable fact that the more one focuses upon oneself and one's emotions (which self-centered people are more than happy to do), the greater the "pile of spaghetti" she is going to create. The psychological community has led people to so disproportionately fixate their attention on human emotions that they then struggle to see beyond them to their real problem. Focusing on human emotions will always stop short of addressing and correcting a person's real problem because the emotions themselves are symptomatic of a deeper sin issue. And psychotherapy provides an environment where every feeling is examined and scrutinized in great detail. All kinds of theories are suggested as to why the woman is doing what she is doing. This is the line of reasoning that ushers in excuses for one's sinful behavior.

Allow me (Kathy) to offer a recent example of this kind of thinking. I was invited by a group of Christian psychotherapists to participate in a meeting regarding sexual sin. The subject of overeating came up. All kinds of reasons were suggested as to why people overeat: "unmet needs," "emotional pain," "medicating oneself through food," etc. Finally, I asked incredulously, "Can't it simply be that people are overeating because their love of food has gotten out of control?"

That question perfectly delineates the difference between God's approach to sin and the answers advanced by humanistic psychology. To those who want to assign responsibility for addictive behavior upon unmet emotional needs, a question such as the one I posed seems simplistic and naïve. In their minds, behind every human dilemma lies a complex combination of contributing factors that must be analyzed.

No such thinking is found anywhere in Scripture. The truth is that we have a sinful nature and therefore love sin. Jeremiah said,

"The heart is deceitful above all things, and desperately wicked: who can know it?" (Jeremiah 17:9 KJV) David said, "Behold, I was brought forth in iniquity, and in sin my mother conceived me." (Psalm 51:5) Solomon remarked, "Foolishness is bound up in the heart of a child." (Proverbs 22:15) Paul claimed that we have all sinned and fallen short of the glory of God (Romans 3:23), while John said that "if we say we have no sin we deceive ourselves." (I John 1:8) And finally, Jesus declared, "But the things that proceed out of the mouth come from the heart, and those defile the man. For out of the heart come evil thoughts, murders, adulteries, fornications, thefts, false witness, slanders. These are the things which defile the man." (Matthew 15:18-20)

As sinners, we crave the temporal pleasures of sin that appeal to our carnal natures. Though not everyone struggles with the *same* sin, every individual has sin that comes naturally. It is this innate attraction for the forbidden that habitual sexual sin stems from.

One of the inevitable consequences to a woman giving over to sin is that she will become increasingly warped in her thinking. Sin brings misery, guilt and shame. A myriad of complex emotional problems will inevitably result from regularly acting out just one form of sinful behavior. It also causes all kinds of problems in our relationships with others. The answer then is not to attempt to deal with the fluctuating emotions that result from the sin, but to go one step deeper and rid oneself of the behavior that is bringing about all of the other secondary problems. Feelings follow behavior. And emotional problems will not be corrected until the woman repents of the sin that causes them.

Dealing With the Roots

When looking for the roots of sexual addiction we do not need to look any further than our own sinful natures. The truth is that the problem is rather simple: by giving over to sin, people become increasingly prideful and self-centered. Much of our lives have been dictated by these two base motives. It is time to come to grips with what truly lies beneath the addict's lack of control. In a nutshell, as she has indulged the desires of her flesh, pride and selfishness have flourished within her. The more she gives her flesh what it demands, the stronger the sin grows within.

Dealing with sexual addiction in the Christian's life can be compared to dealing with bedsores of those suffering from debilitating illnesses. You can treat these painful lesions with the latest ointments, creams, and bandages, but unless you cure the disease, the patient will stay bedridden and continue to suffer with such irritation.

In the same way, habitual sexual sin is a by-product of a self-centered lifestyle. The woman is addicted to illicit sex *because* she is consumed with herself. You can "treat" the sexual problem for the rest of your life, but until the selfish nature is dealt with, the propensity to sin will remain. This is the reason Pure Life Ministries puts an emphasis on dealing with *all* the aspects of a believer's spiritual life. As the believer matures as a Christian, he or she will become increasingly more interested in the lives of others. The less *self*-centered she becomes, the less important *self*-gratification will be in her life.

The Death Process

Once a woman is born-again, God immediately begins a process of renewal in her life—changing her into a "new creation." (II Corinthians 5:17 NIV) However, her response or willingness to allow God to reshape her into the likeness of His Son, Jesus Christ, is vitally important if she hopes to mature spiritually and walk in daily victory over her sin. Christians grow at different rates, depending upon their willingness to cooperate with the work of the Holy Spirit within them. The Lord begins to methodically strip away all the characteristics of self. The less of self that is present, the more room there is for the Personhood of Jesus to shine through. As the woman learns to die to self, she becomes increasingly more Christ-like—and increasingly more free of the bondages that are part of her self-life.

God may use many kinds of experiences in our lives to bring about this transformation. We are all familiar with Romans 8:28 and often use it whenever things go badly. However, this verse is often taken out of context. It is the next verse that is the key: "And we know that God causes all things to work together for good to those who love God, to those who are called according to *His purpose*. For whom He foreknew, He also predestined to become *conformed to the image of His Son…*" The key words in this section of Scripture are "His purpose." God's purpose for His children is that they "become conformed to the image of His Son." Hence, all things (i.e. circumstances, trials, reproof, discipline, etc.) are meant to bring about this divine inward change. God desires to mold us into "extensions" of Jesus to be dispersed throughout the earth as His vessels of mercy. Our part in this process is to learn to "die to self" so that God can have free reign to make us more like Jesus Christ.

Denying Self

What all people in sexual sin share in common is a lack of self-control. They have been unable to rein in their sexual urges. They have never learned how to "deny" themselves. In fact, many have obsessively pursued pleasure to the point that they have uncaringly sacrificed their walk with God, their marriages, and their families in the process. Fulfilling their every desire has been their number one priority. However, Jesus said, "If anyone wishes to come after Me, let him deny himself, and take up his cross daily, and follow Me. For whoever wishes to save his life shall lose it, but whoever loses his life for My sake, he is the one who will save it." (Luke 9:23-24)

In addressing the prevalent lie, "I need to learn to love myself," Nancy DeMoss writes:

> [This] is the world's prescription for those who are plagued with a sense of worthlessness. It has become a popular mantra of pop psychology and of a culture filled with people obsessed with finding ways to feel better about themselves...
>
> The fact is, we do not hate ourselves, nor do we need to learn to love ourselves. We need to learn how to deny ourselves, so we can do that which does not come naturally—to truly love God and others. Our malady is not "low self-esteem," nor is it how we view ourselves; rather, it is our low view of God.[8]

Overcoming habits of sexual sin requires more than simply exercising self-control, otherwise it would not be called an addiction. The woman fighting such a battle must learn to say "no" when temptations arise. Yet, there is still more.

The woman walking in victory is one who has learned to "deny self." This must become a way of life. Indeed, Jesus requires this of *all* who profess to be followers of His. Denying self means that we must lay aside our self-serving and self-gratifying desires in favor of God's will. Such obedience is gradually worked into the woman who willingly submits to God's discipline, allowing Him to govern and rule her life.

We have found that most people who are addicted to one particular thing also fail to exercise control in other areas of their lives. For instance, overeating is very common among women who are involved in sexual sin. Others run up credit card bills, disregarding the inevitable consequences. Still others indulge in entertainment or any number of frivolous pursuits. Often this occurs because the underlying problem is not sexual addiction, but rather the overall lack of control, restraint, and discipline that comes from a life of self-gratification. One of the keys to overcoming an addiction is to learn restraint in *every* area of life; not just the area of the addiction. As the woman learns moderation in other aspects of life, she will find that the temptation to indulge in sexual sin will be weakened. Pursuing other forms of pleasure only serves to strengthen the addiction because gratifying oneself simply reinforces self-centeredness.

Taking up one's cross, as Jesus commanded in Luke 9:23, means putting an end to the old nature—the self-life. Calvary represents death to the old way of living. As Paul said, "Therefore, if anyone is in Christ, he is a new creation; the old has gone, the new has come!" (II Corinthians 5:17 NIV) Something should be drastically different in the woman who has come to Christ. There should be a fundamental and noticeable change in her nature. The Cross of Calvary represents the end of an old era and the ushering in of a new. We especially like A.W. Tozer's depiction of this:

> The old cross is a symbol of death. It stands for the abrupt, violent end of a human being. The man in Roman times who took up his cross and started down the road had already said good-bye to his friends. He was not coming back. He was going out to have it ended. The cross made no compromise, modified nothing, spared nothing; it slew all of the man, completely and for good. It did not try to keep on good terms with its victim. It struck cruel and hard, and when it had finished its work, the man was no more.[9]

Pride—The Cancer of the Soul

The other root of sexual sin is pride. Solomon said, "Pride goes before destruction and a haughty spirit before a fall." (Proverbs 16:18) It seems that the more prideful a woman is, the more difficult overcoming sexual sin becomes. Pride is simply being filled with self and a sense of one's own importance. The greater the self-life, the more prominent pride will be within a woman. This attitude must be seriously dealt with if a woman hopes to overcome self and her consequent sexual sin.

We have identified several distinct manifestations of pride.*** Every person alive deals with one or more of these sinful attitudes.

A woman with a haughty spirit is one who considers herself to be superior to others around her. She often treats people with disdain. The woman with self-protective pride fortifies herself with an elaborate system of walls and defense mechanisms, in an attempt to keep herself from vulnerability. The person with unapproachable pride cannot be corrected, reproved, or confronted on any matter. Vanity is being excessively concerned about the way one looks to others. The woman with know-it-all pride has a super-inflated view of her own abilities and therefore resists being taught by others. Self-exalting pride is at the root of the "Worship Me" attitude discussed in Chapter Three: wanting to be the center of attention or affection, regardless of who may get brushed aside in the process. The woman who has unsubmissive pride is rebellious to authority and arrogantly places herself at the same level as her leaders. Lastly, the woman with spiritual pride exaggerates her spirituality, seeing herself way beyond her actual level of godliness.

The Way Out Is Down

Genuine humility is a fruit of the Spirit that comes from true brokenness—the breaking down process of self. The more of the old nature that remains in a believer, the less room there is for Christ or His attributes. Andrew Murray said, "This is the true

---

*** The evil nature of pride is much more exhaustively addressed in the author's book, *Irresistible to God.*

self-denial to which our Savior calls us—the acknowledgment that self has nothing good in it except as an empty vessel which God must fill. It is simply *the sense of entire nothingness, which comes when we see how truly God is all, and in which we make way for God to be all.*"[10] (Emphasis in original)

It is not a matter of having high self-esteem or low self-esteem. Anyone who matures as a believer will eventually come to the place where *self*-esteem is replaced with *Christ's* esteem. A woman does not combat the low opinion she may have of herself by trying to pump herself up. The only real answer for a woman struggling with (so-called) "low self esteem," is to humble herself and allow the Lord to infuse a sense of assurance and fulfillment that comes to any child of God who is walking in obedience to Him. Drawing nearer to the Lord results in a corresponding decrease in self-awareness, which is vital to achieving lowliness of mind through the guidance of the Holy Spirit.

One of the themes of the New Testament is servanthood. Oh, how foreign this concept is in the Church today! It is not lowliness that most desire, but loftiness! Striving for honor is such a part of our human nature that it seems practically unavoidable. Even the disciples, during the very eve of our Savior's crucifixion, argued amongst themselves about who was the greatest. Jesus answered them and said, "Let him who is the greatest among you become the servant." (Luke 22:26) After saying this, He got on His hands and knees and washed their feet. The Lord was showing them, through this act of total servitude and selflessness, how to be a servant. He said, "You call me Teacher and Lord; and you are right, for so I am. If I then, the Lord and the Teacher, washed your feet, you also should do as I did to you. Truly, truly I say to you, a slave is not greater than his master; if you know these things, you are blessed if you do them." (John 13:13-15)

The point Jesus was making was not that we should have foot-washing ceremonies, although there might be a place for that. Rather, He was showing believers that His Kingdom is one made up of servants.

Becoming a servant is a mindset that a person must develop. It involves a lifestyle of putting others before oneself. Pride and self-centeredness are so intertwined in the fabric of our beings that it is virtually impossible to deal with one without dealing with the other. Until a woman learns to put others before herself, she will never truly be free from the desire to gratify her selfish flesh. Humbling oneself by acts of servitude is one of the greatest tools God has given us to overcome the self-life. Self-centeredness is the foundation that sexual sin thrives upon. Living in an awareness of the needs of others and having a servant's heart will absolutely undermine the self-centered life and counteract the powerful temptation of lust for more of that which is forbidden.

CHAPTER SEVEN:
THE NEED TO LIVE IN THE LIGHT

*"When I did not confess my sins, I was worn out
from crying all day long." (Psalm 32:3 GNB)*

A s we have already seen, there is a growing number of Christian girls and women who have quietly become addicted to pornography and/or various forms of sexual sin. While this problem will only escalate in the days ahead, it will, to a large degree, remain hidden under the surface. There are numerous reasons why these women will maintain secrecy about their sin.

First, sexual sin is shameful to admit for anybody but especially for a woman. In our society, a single young man may be glorified for being a "Don Juan," but this is not the case for a girl. If a woman admits her struggles to her pastor, from that day on she will wonder what her pastor thinks of her: "Is he thinking I'm lusting over him? Is he concerned about me being a bad influence on others? Was that sermon about lust aimed at me? Has he told others in the church about my problem?" These concerns make it difficult for the struggling believer to confide in her pastor, let alone others in the church.

Secondly, even though our society does not consider fornication or even adultery to be shameful, these sins are considered big "no-no's" in the evangelical movement. A woman can have a terrible habit of spreading gossip in the church; she can be obsessed with her work at the expense of her children; or she can be extremely critical of those around her, but these, as well as many other sins, are overlooked in the Church. However, if a woman admits to committing adultery, she is instantly judged as someone who is far from God. In this regard, our corporate attitude is really not all that different from the Pharisees in John 8 who were ready to stone to death the woman (and not the man) who was caught in the act of adultery. We still maintain the same double standard today.

Another factor that contributes to a woman keeping her sin covered is that it is fairly easy to live a double life of outward religion and secret sexual sin. Unlike alcohol or drug abuse, a woman can maintain an outwardly normal life without being discovered. There is a lifestyle that goes with getting high. Drugs and alcohol affect a person's ability to function. Few are able to keep this kind of a habit secret. But with sexual addiction, a woman can be a pastor's wife or even a celebrity and still maintain an outward façade of respectability. Consider the following comments made by a woman who responded to the survey we recently conducted on our website.

> Women love sex and many of us are visually aroused like men. I feel it is easier to get away with it because I am a woman. No one suspects that a woman could be involved in this. Now with the Internet it makes it too easy for women to get caught up in porn online and nobody knows. I don't want to have this problem, but I learned as a teen to lie very well and I still can lie very easily to my husband, children, others—even myself. Many times I want to cleanse myself and my mind of the thoughts, images and things I have seen or done, but just don't feel there is a place to do that. Also, if I admit it to someone that would mean I would be held accountable—sometimes I want that, sometimes I don't. I am 38 years old and have struggled for most of 27 years—mostly in silence.

When the Inward and Outward Do Not Line Up

We all have an inside world that is made up of the different parts of what the Bible calls our *inner man*: the heart, soul, mind, spirit, will, intellect and emotions. It is the life that goes on inside of us: our thoughts, feelings, attitudes, sentiments and opinions. This is where dreams are born and failures grieved, the place where intricate processes are put into motion and life's decisions are contemplated. Here we also find the conflicting emotions of love and hate, like and dislike, attraction and repulsion. Our inside world is where we live our daily existence. Some people are considered "open" because they are not afraid to show their thoughts and feelings with other people. Others are thought to be "closed," feeling anxious when people become too intimate. Regardless of how willing a person is to talk about his or her feelings, the truth is, we will never completely allow another to intimately know the deepest part of our inner man. This is an extremely private place, an inner sanctum—a holy of holies, so to speak.

The outward life stands in contrast to the inside world. This is how we speak and act in front of other people. We all have an image which we attempt to maintain—a way in which we want other people to view us. One person might want to be seen as someone who is intellectual and cultured. Another might want to portray herself as being a good mom, while yet another will want to be seen as sweet. The impressions we wish to project are woven into everything we say and do in the presence of other people.

The tendency to project ourselves the way we want others to view us also carries over into the spiritual life, where we encounter the overwhelming temptation to make ourselves appear in a favorable light. If we are Christians surrounded by other Christians, we tend to project ourselves as being "spiritual." Why? In Christian circles, looking "spiritual" is what causes others to admire and respect us. For someone to admit fault, defeat or (horror of horrors) flagrant sin, would be to admit to being a failure at Christianity.

Because Jesus understood the fears people wrestle with, He took the time to address this issue one day. Turning to His closest followers, He gave them this sober warning:

> "Beware of the leaven of the Pharisees, which is hypocrisy. But there is nothing covered up that will not be revealed, and hidden that will not be known. Accordingly, whatever you have said in the dark shall be heard in the light, and what you have whispered in the inner rooms shall be proclaimed upon the housetops. And I say to you, My friends, do not be afraid of those who kill the body, and after that have no more that they can do. But I will warn you whom to fear: fear the One who after He has killed has authority to cast into hell; yes, I tell you, fear Him!" (Luke 12:1-5)

The best present-day analogy to this admonition would be the warning signs one encounters along a highway: "CAUTION!" "WARNING!" "STOP!" "DANGER!" Jesus' use of such a strong term as "beware" shows how extremely hazardous He considered hypocrisy to be.

We all have, to some degree, a fear of what other people think of us. Presumably it begins on the playground where kids can be so cruel to one another. The fear is deepened during the awkward teenage years and becomes embedded during adulthood. Jesus says that we must overcome these fears and instead concentrate our fears upon God, "the One who after He has killed has authority to cast into hell; yes, I tell you, fear Him!" In other words, we should be more concerned about the reality of our inward spiritual condition than how we look outwardly in the eyes of others.

The conflict between the way we present ourselves outwardly

and the way we live our lives inwardly is a predominant theme in Scripture. Paul said, "For he is not a Jew who is one outwardly; neither is circumcision that which is outward in the flesh. But he is a Jew who is one inwardly; and circumcision is that which is of the heart, by the Spirit, not by the letter; and his praise is not from men, but from God." (Romans 2:28-29) God said through the prophet Isaiah, "These people come near to me with their mouth and honor me with their lips, but their hearts are far from me. Their worship of me is made up only of rules taught by men." (Isaiah 29:13 NIV) And to the prophet Samuel He said, "God sees not as man sees, for man looks at the outward appearance, but the LORD looks at the heart." (I Samuel 16:7) And, as we have already seen, Peter told the Christian women of his day, "Your beauty should not come from outward adornment, such as braided hair and the wearing of gold jewelry and fine clothes. Instead, it should be that of your inner self, the unfading beauty of a gentle and quiet spirit, which is of great worth in God's sight." (I Peter 3:3-4 NIV)

There are over two thousand direct references to the inner life in the Bible, but it is indirectly referred to on almost every page. It is clear that Scripture places an enormous emphasis on what goes on inside us. Many Christians today closely resemble the Pharisees addressed by Jesus in Luke 11:39, who "…clean the outside of the cup and of the platter; but inside of [them, they] are full of robbery and wickedness." In essence, they ignore the importance of the inward life and choose to concentrate on presenting the most favorable outward appearance.

The Apostle John also observed this happening around him. In his first epistle, he said the following in regard to this dichotomy:

> If *we say* that we have fellowship with Him and yet walk in the darkness, we lie and do not practice the truth; but if we walk in the light as He Himself is in

	What we say	What we do	Results or reality of situation
vs. 6	we have fellowship with Him	walk in darkness	we lie; do not practice truth
vs. 7	----------------	walk in light	we have fellowship; blood of Jesus cleanses us
vs. 8	we have no sin	deceive ourselves	truth is not in us
vs. 9	confess our sin	----------------	He forgives and cleanses us
vs. 10	we have not sinned	make Him a liar	The word is not in us

Figure 7-1

the light, we have fellowship with one another, and the blood of Jesus His Son cleanses us from all sin. If *we say* that we have no sin, we are deceiving ourselves, and the truth is not in us. If we confess our sins, He is faithful and righteous to forgive us our sins and to cleanse us from all unrighteousness. If *we say* that we have not sinned, we make Him a liar, and His word is not in us. (I John 1:6-10)

In the chart above, we can see a breakdown of those verses in John's epistle. There are three categories. The first, *what we say*, is simply what we convey to those around us. The second classification is *what we do*. Our actions speak of our true condition, what we are really like. The third category describes the *result,* the consequence of what we say and what we do. When a person blameshifts, minimizes or conceals her sin, the message she sends to those around her is that she has no sin. Of course, she may never actually say the words, "I have no sin." she simply tries to convince others of her innocence by masking it or minimizing it. When John wrote these words he was simply referring to all Christians. Everyone certainly has some degree of sin—no one is exempt. Those who are in unrepentant sexual sin are all the more guilty of hypocrisy because their sin is much deeper than that of the average believer.

John clearly shows us how vitally important it is to bring our sin into the "light" through open confession. The Greek word for confession, *homologeo*, literally means "to be of one mind, to bring oneself into agreement with another." Whether or not we acknowledge (to ourselves or to others) that our sin is present, it still exists and God sees it. When we confess our sin, or "walk in the light," the blood of Christ graciously cleanses us from guilt, and we come into fellowship with the believer we opened up to. It is not enough for a person to come to grips with her sin. She must come into the light with others. Darkness is the devil's domain. Those who refuse to come into the light about their sin are choosing to remain in darkness.

Exposure

The Christian woman who thinks she can continue hiding her sin will eventually discover that God loves her too much to allow her to maintain her secret sin. It may become evident in her speech, mannerisms or some other way, but at some point, her secret life will be exposed to those around her. Jesus promised this when He said, "For nothing is hidden that shall not become evident, nor anything secret that shall not be known and come to light." (Luke 8:17)

The Christian woman who is involved in sexual sin will only be able to hide her true identity for so long. God has been known to bring public humiliation upon one of His children in order to get his or her attention. If He feels that He needs to do so, He will. He is very patient and gentle with us, but He loves us too much to leave us in our sin.

This was the case for a woman who was having an adulterous affair with her pastor. One day, as they were engaged in a sexual conversation on the phone, the pastor somehow inadvertently flipped on the intercom button. The whole conversation ended up being broadcast throughout the church. Both were publicly humiliated and the pastor was forced to resign his position. Later the woman could look back and see how God had repeatedly tried to get her attention, but to no avail. God will not strive with a person forever!

The Deception of Sexual Sin

People are prone to overlook their deeply embedded sin because it has an extremely deceptive nature. There exists an interesting correlation between a person's involvement with sin and her awareness of it. The more a woman becomes involved in sin, the less she sees it. Sin is a hideous disease that destroys a person's ability to comprehend its existence. It could be compared to a computer virus that has the ability to hide its presence from the user while it systematically destroys the hard drive. Typically, those who are the most entangled in sin are the very ones who cannot see its presence at work inside them. Sin has the ability to mask itself so well that it can actually make the woman who deals with it the least, think she is the most spiritual.

On the other hand, the more a woman overcomes sin in her life and draws closer to God, the more glaringly her *nature of sin* stands out. God "dwells in unapproachable light" (I Timothy 6:16) and so consequently, every remnant of selfishness, pride, and sin is going to be exposed to the sincere seeker. The intense, brilliant light of God exposes what is in a person's heart. Those who want to draw near to Him rejoice because of this. They love the Light and so they embrace it, even though it means their true selves will be unmasked. Jesus said, "And this is the judgment, that the light is come into the world, and men loved the darkness rather than the light; for their deeds were evil. For everyone who does evil hates the light, and does not come to the light, lest his deeds should be exposed. But he who practices the truth comes to the light, that his deeds may be manifested as having been wrought in God." (John 3:19-21)

If a woman who is bound by sexual sin hopes to turn her

life around, it is crucial that she comes into the light with "the sin which doth so easily beset" her, so that she may finally "lay aside every weight" and walk in victory through Jesus Christ. (Hebrews 12:1 KJV)

If it appears that we are promoting the idea that one should walk around berating herself or beating herself down, nothing could be further from the truth. We are however, advocating the need for a woman to come into reality about where she is spiritually. Her only hope is to have something real in God. Keeping herself hyped up in a false sense of security will only keep her buried under the burden of unconfessed sin, which in turn will further the delusion about her spirituality.

The application which men must complete for the Pure Life Ministries Live-In Program for sexual addicts asks the following:

Please rate yourself on a scale of 1 to 10 in the following areas (10 being very godly and 1 being very carnal):

Loving others___ Relationship to God___ Prayer Life___ Obedience___ Humility___
Generosity___ Kindness___ Joy___ Self-Discipline___ Zeal___ Maturity___ Honesty___

Men who come to us for help are often struggling with the deepest perversions imaginable. With this in mind, it would probably surprise you to see how they rate themselves spiritually. Typically, the applicants rate themselves fairly high on everything except self-discipline. It is not uncommon to see six's, seven's, and even eight's across the board in their self-evaluation. How can this be? The majority of them come into the program thinking of themselves as being fairly godly people with only "one small problem."

It takes months of patient work on the part of our counselors to help a man see that he is not as godly as he has thought he was and that there is much work to be done in his life. It is only then that his hardened heart begins to soften, and he finally sees his need for the Lord. The attitude he entered the program with, believing that he was fairly godly with only one small problem, gradually dissipates, and we can begin to help him. Why is it so important for him to come to this realization? If he believes that he is in fairly good shape spiritually, he will not see his need to change, grow, mature, or even repent. We have occasionally had to ask men who have come to the program with such an attitude, "If you're so godly and have it so together, why are you seeking our help?" This question is not meant to insult them, but it quickly brings them into some semblance of reality; humility is now produced so that we can begin to lead them onto the path of victory.

However, when people continually minimize the sin in their lives, they are only deceiving themselves. J.C. Ryle wrote of the deceitfulness of sin:

> You may see this deceitfulness in the wonderful proneness of men to regard sin as less sinful and dangerous than it is in the sight of God and in their readiness to extenuate it, make excuses for it and minimize its guilt...You may see it in the long string of smooth words and phrases which men have coined in order to designate things which God calls downright wicked and ruinous to the soul...men try to cheat themselves into the belief that sin is not quite so sinful as God says it is, and that they are not so bad as they really are.[1]

Living in the Light

Being honest is an extremely important issue for the woman struggling with sexual sin. Honesty begins with examining one's own heart, thought life, and actions. In this process, the sincere woman will humble and brace herself for the unavoidable conclusion: "I am not nearly as godly as I imagined myself to be. If I'm ever going to change, I must quit fooling myself and others. I am where I am, spiritually. Keeping an inflated perspective of my spirituality is only hindering any real growth. The truth is that my heart is full of wickedness. My thinking has become increasingly warped. I have hurt God and my family by my actions. I need to do whatever it takes to change."

Being brutally honest with oneself is crucial, but it is only the beginning. One man who had been convicted for attempted rape but later struggled his way out of sexual addiction said, "If you don't want to get rid of the problem, confess it only to God. If you want to get rid of the problem, confess it to another person. And if you *really* want to get rid of the problem, keep yourself accountable!" Yet another man who is now living in victory said, "I confessed my sin to God for years. I mean I poured my heart out, begging for His forgiveness, but it was within weeks of starting to confess to another brother, that I obtained victory!"

A woman who is struggling needs to be honest with herself and at least one other woman. That woman should be a godly Christian who is strong in the Word. She should also be the kind of woman who is willing to lovingly confront the confessor about her sin as well as encourage her in her growth in righteousness.

There is great healing in confession (James 5:16), and it only benefits a woman in her commitment to change. Just knowing that there is someone who is aware of her secret life and is exhorting her toward victory is a tremendous help. Solomon said, "He who conceals his transgressions will not prosper, but he who confesses and forsakes them will find compassion." (Proverbs 28:13)

The double life must be dismantled no matter what. Satan knows the power he has within secrecy. The woman who wants to remain in her sin avoids exposure at all cost. However, the woman who is serious about overcoming it exposes her sin so that she is less likely to succumb to the temptations when they arise later. Living a double life prevents a solid foundation of godliness from being formed. James said that the double-minded man is "unstable in all of his ways." (James 1:8) This woman will never experience real spiritual stability.

We have heard people tell us many times that they do not have anyone to confess to. What they were really saying is that they were not desperate enough to seek out someone that might be able to assist them. If a woman is determined to break free from the hold of sexual sin, she will do whatever it takes. Making oneself transparent to another person is one of the difficult things that *must* be done. A woman may institute all of the other steps outlined in this book into her life, but if she hedges on this one, all other efforts might prove to have been in vain.

We must ask the question (we will discuss in detail in Chapter 9): "How much do you care?" When you get to the place that you are truly sick of the sin in your life, will you be willing to do *anything*, even making yourself vulnerable to another person? What could stop you? Only the desire to save face, to save reputation, and protect self. *Real deliverance from sexual sin can never be possible until the heart is opened up and exposed.* Glossing over, hiding and masking one's true inner person will only keep oneself locked into darkness.

Find someone in your church to open up to. If you do not know who would be best, go to your pastor's wife and explain to her that you want to make yourself accountable to someone and ask her for guidance to identify who would be most trustworthy. You will find that ongoing accountability will prove to be a very important step in the overcoming process.

Secondly, if you are a married woman it is important to open up to your husband. In dealing with male sexual addicts, we have often had men tell us that they could not bear to hurt their wives who are unaware of their problem. We can only reply,

"If you were all that concerned about your wife, you wouldn't have committed the sin in the first place. And not only that, but it's your sin that is hurting your wife. She may not know about it, but you are destroying your home because of it." Truthfully, the man is not concerned about hurting his wife as much as he is about making the painful confession to her of what he is really like. It is not the *knowledge* of the sin that is hurting his wife but the sin itself!

The same advice applies to women. In countless different ways, a woman with illicit sex in her life hurts her loved ones. Yes, truth hurts, but the pain of the truth is far more preferable than the pain of sin when one compares the consequences of both. Hiding their sin is just another way that the self-centered lifestyle of sexual addicts manifests itself. In truth, they are far more concerned about the cost they will have to pay for their transparency than the possible harm done to loved ones.

True Biblical Accountability

As we mentioned before, bringing secret sin into the open is vital. But biblical accountability was never meant to be a group of Christians sitting in a circle discussing their failures. Such a setting may be somewhat helpful to believers who need to bring their sin out into the open with others, but there is no power in such a situation to bring about their needed deliverance.

A person can only lead another spiritually as far as she has gone herself. Jesus said, "…if a blind man guides a blind man, both will fall into a pit." (Matthew 15:14) It is helpful to a certain extent to open up with other people about one's struggles. But there is a biblical principle that is far more powerful in its ability to change lives. What women greatly need is to be discipled. "What do you mean? I've read all the Christian self-help books. I've heard the best sermons on Christian radio. I just need a little bit of accountability!"

It might surprise the reader to find out that the word "accountability" is not mentioned once in the Bible. The concept is in Scripture, but not in the weak way in which it is currently used today. Instead, the biblical concept is that of being discipled. We are not referring to receiving more information about Christianity. Listening to good sermons and reading interesting books can be helpful, but what the immature Christian needs most is for a mature woman to take her under her wing, so to speak, and bring godly instruction into her life. (This is what we do for men and women in our counseling programs at Pure Life Ministries.) The spiritual growth that is necessary for the woman who is in the grip of sin will not come about by simply talking with other struggling women, nor will it come by acquiring more head knowledge on the subject. It only comes through true discipleship—Christ-centered discipleship.

Jesus had those occasions when He spoke to the multitudes, but He spent enormous amounts of time building spiritual character into the small group of men under His care. A woman may hear sermons, but unless she is held accountable to respond to those words, she will probably receive little benefit from what was said. The woman is lost in a crowd of listeners. She can ignore, disregard, even disagree with what she is hearing, and is never required to face the truth of what is being stated.

However, when a godly woman dedicates herself to discipling the struggling Christian sister, something powerful happens. Truth is imparted. Sin is dealt with head on. The mentor expects change. Most importantly, the woman experiences firsthand someone who is walking in the light and confronting her. This is the biblical pattern for accountability. It seems that in the busy lifestyle Americans live, spiritual leaders no longer have the time to mentor others as they once did. Sin is running rampant in the Church because Christians can now live out their lives without any true accountability for their actions.

CHAPTER EIGHT

FREEDOM COMES SLOWLY
FOR A REASON

*"Therefore we do not lose heart, but though our
outer man is decaying, yet our inner man is being
renewed day by day. For momentary, light affliction
is producing for us an eternal weight of glory far
beyond all comparison." (II Corinthians 4:16-17)*

God transforms a woman in two distinct ways: either
through a miracle, which occurs instantaneously, or
through a process of change over an extended period
of time. Many drug addicts who persisted in their habits for years,
have been set free instantly upon coming to the Lord. God does
not always choose to deal with them in this manner, although we
have heard of many cases in which He has done so.

However, the Lord almost always deals with those in sexual
sin through a gradual, well-organized process of transforming
the woman into a new creation. In all our years of counseling
sexual addicts, we could count on one hand those who were
instantly delivered.

Just as it has usually taken a woman years to entangle herself
in such a spiritual mess, it will take some time for her to work her
way out of it. In today's "microwave" society, in which people
get cured of their ailments quickly, we have become accustomed
to expecting immediate results for everything we desire. As a

result, people often get impatient with God's timetable. As we will explore in this chapter, you will see there are good reasons why change does not typically happen quickly.

One of the things we must realize is that if God were to instantly set us free, it would then be much easier for us to return to old habits. However, when a woman has to fight and struggle to break the powerful grip of sin, she will appreciate the freedom she eventually experiences.

In 1982, when the two of us came to the Lord and decided to quit smoking, we set a date to quit and prepared ourselves for a great battle. We planned to spend the day hiking, hoping to alleviate some of the tremendous amount of stress we expected. When the day finally came, it was almost a disappointment. There was no battle. It was too easy! A few weeks later I (Steve) found myself in a stressful situation on my job as a deputy working in the jail. Another deputy was smoking a cigarette, and I was tempted to have one too. I remember thinking that quitting smoking was easy, so why not? I started smoking again, but the next time I quit I had to work for it!

So it was for my sexual addiction. All of the pain Kathy and I have endured has had a real effect on me. It has enabled me to see the consequences of my sin more clearly. During those times of battling the temptations of sexual sin, I became determined to resist them, partly because of the price I had already paid. I simply did not want to have to pay such a price again; I knew the end result all too well.

There is a second benefit that comes from having to endure a slower, more gradual process of obtaining freedom from sexual sin. Through this painstaking, reshaping process God is teaching the woman to totally rely on Him. God is a master craftsman and actually *uses* a woman's sin to eventually draw her closer to Himself. The consequences of a woman's sin are often instrumental in driving her to her knees so that she will desperately cry out to the Lord for help. Being utterly powerless over sin makes a woman dependent upon God. If she could quit her sin in herself why would she then need the Lord? Consequently, God uses circumstances to teach the woman to fully rely on Him and to convince her of the truth the Psalmist wrote, "...deliverance by man is in vain." (Psalm 60:11)

God's Timing

One should also realize that God will deal with a woman in His own timing. He knows when each person is prepared for the next step in the journey to freedom. The woman dealing with sexual sin can often see no further than that seemingly insurmountable sin in her life. She wants to be freed of her sin and the suffering associated with it. Yet God sees her heart and her entire future. He knows there are many deeply-rooted issues which must be exposed and subsequently dealt with. God is often more concerned about exposing and expelling the underlying issues of the heart than He is about the outward sin with which she struggles. Since the woman is looking to Him for help, the Lord is able to use this critical period of her life to uncover other areas which are aiding and abetting her unremitting addiction to sex.

Oblivious to the fact that God has even greater plans for her life, the woman bound up in habitual sin is inclined to be preoccupied simply with being set free. Delivering her out of the clutches of her sexual sin is only part of what the Lord desires to do in her life, though. For instance, the lack of love the woman shows for those around her might seem to be a secondary issue, but it is a matter of extreme importance to the Lord. Yes, He wants to see her delivered, but He is also concerned about her character once she has been set free from her sin. Will her selfishness simply be transferred to spending money? Will she live out the rest of her life with no concern for the lost who are going to hell around her? Will she continue to be self-centered with her family? As the writer of Hebrews exhorts us: "…let us lay aside *every* weight, and the sin which doth so easily beset us." (Hebrews 12:1 KJV) As was discussed in Chapter Six, the underlying problem of habitual sin is self-centeredness. God desires to use this season in the woman's life to work on her selfish and prideful nature. The woman in sin often sees no further than the immediate freedom she desires, but the Lord looks at the long term results.

As the woman goes through the process of restoration, God tries to birth and cultivate the fruit of the Spirit. He expects her to possess a great godly love for others. The Lord wants to see her life filled with the true peace and joy which comes only from the Spirit. He teaches her the enormous value of being patient with other people. During this period of time, He also builds up her faith and instills goodness into her. And yes, He even develops in her the divine self-control which can withstand the temptations of the enemy.

However, a life transformed from one of corruption and utter uselessness to one of fruitfulness and purpose, is not spared the experience of pain. Deliverance from habitual sin also involves personal loss. A true overcomer must part with certain relationships, places, and things that were intimately associated with her sinful lifestyle. This can be extremely difficult and often traumatic to the woman who, for many years, has looked to her sin for comfort, pleasure, and as an escape from the real world. The woman invariably finds herself grieving the loss of—not just the pleasure of the sin—but also the other elements which accompanied the lifestyle of that sin. The truth is, the idolatry of sexual sin has stolen God's rightful place in her life, causing her to turn to her idol as a reason for life and to always run to it for comfort. It has become a sanctuary from the pain of reality. *She has worshiped at its altar for many years.*

Learning to Fight

There is an aspect to Christianity described in the Book of Revelation that must be mentioned here. In chapters 2 and 3, John is instructed to write letters to seven churches which were located in the province of Asia. These seven letters cover all of the general struggles churches have encountered through the centuries. One phrase is repeated at the end of each letter: "To him who overcomes…" Seven different aspects of eternal life are then promised for each overcoming church.

The Greek word which we translate as "overcomes" is *nikao*, which means to conquer or subdue. It comes from the root word *nike*, meaning victory. Thus, we learn that Christians are meant to conquer or subdue something. Some synonyms for the word conquer are *surmount, prevail against, subjugate, master* and *overpower*. These terms describe the kind of life the believer is expected to live and experience.

Throughout her Christian journey, the woman will constantly be faced with obstacles to living a holy life. As we will discuss later, most of these hindrances lie within her own flesh. Others are placed in her path by the spirit of this world. Whatever the source of opposition, she is expected to overcome these snares. Paul spoke of "fighting the good fight," (I Timothy 1:18; 6:12) "waging war," (Romans 7:23) "weapons of our warfare," (II Corinthians 10:4) "our struggle" (Ephesians 6:12) and being a "soldier in active service." (II Timothy 2:4) Peter said we should "abstain from fleshly lusts, which wage war against the soul." (I Peter 2:11) James stated that it is "your pleasures that wage war in your members." (James 4:1) There is no question that the woman must learn to battle against her own carnal desires and the temptations presented by the enemy.

The Old Testament illustration of this is found in the book of Judges. According to Scripture, God actually allowed wicked, demon-worshiping nations to remain in Palestine. The reason: "Now these are the nations which the LORD left, to test Israel by them (that is, all who had not experienced any of the wars of Canaan; only in order that the generations of the sons of Israel might be taught war, those who had not experienced it formerly)." (Judges 3:1-2)

The land of ancient Palestine was full of fertility cults. The Israelites were forced to battle against the people who offered them the very thing that their flesh wanted. Throughout the history of the nation of Israel, the people vacillated back and forth between the worship of Jehovah and the worship of idols. God could have simply rained fire down from heaven upon all of those idolaters, but instead, He told His people to drive them out. This type of mortal combat in the natural epitomizes the battles which are fought in the spiritual realm by the New Testament believer whose weapons "...are not carnal, but mighty through God to the pulling down of strongholds." (II Corinthians 10:4 KJV)

Consequently, the Christian woman bound up in sexual sin must wage war against the enemies of her soul, "Casting down imaginations, and every high thing that exalteth itself against the knowledge of God, and bringing into captivity every thought to the obedience of Christ." (II Corinthians 10:5 KJV) She must strive to abandon the dichotomous love-hate relationship with her sin. Her flesh loves it and wants it to remain, though she understands the evil of it and longs for God to set her free. She cries out to the Lord and then, a day or two later, is right back in the middle of her sin. Rather than giving her an instantaneous deliverance or a desired "quick-fix," the Lord wants her to learn how to battle against it. Why? In order that she learn to hate evil as the Lord does. As any good soldier, the woman who overcomes must stay in the fight to the very end, depending solely on the Lord's help. Eventually, she will truly develop a righteous indignation (i.e. hatred) for her sin and the evils which war against her soul.

How Long Will it Take?

A woman dealing with habitual sexual sin needs to understand that it takes time to overcome entrenched habits of sin. Defeating her addiction will begin only when she accepts the fact that she needs to change her unmanageable sex life. How long it will take essentially depends on two factors. The first is the depth of her involvement with sexual sin. Has she been doing it for years? Has she been in denial over her problem? Has she been refusing to face responsibility for her actions? How deep has she gone into depravity? If there is proof that a deeply-rooted addiction exists, the time it will take to loosen the powerful hold that sin has had on her could be lengthy. In such cases, the addiction has grown so large and has become so deeply ingrained into her very being, that it has become a large part of who she is as a person. It is understandable how frightening it may be for her to relinquish something she identifies as part of her nature.

If her problem has gone no farther than pornography and/or masturbation, then she is fortunate, indeed. Overcoming the habit of masturbation is much easier than conquering a deep-seated addiction such as lesbianism, for instance. The further the woman has gone into the pit of sin, the more difficult will be her climb out. Thus, the more extensive the perversion, the greater the battle will be as God seeks to restore her to sanity.

The other factor is the woman's determination to find freedom at any cost. Our experience has been that it is easier to work with someone who has long-standing problems yet really wants help than a woman whose problems are less severe but is flippant about becoming godly. Sometimes the woman with the worst addiction is the one who finds the greatest freedom. Understanding her need, she knows she *must* find her way to God no matter what. Others put forth little or no effort and never come into real victory.

Still others make victory the center of their lives but look to the wrong places. Take Susan, for instance. Although her problem was not extreme, and though she put much effort into quitting, she has had little result. She determined in her mind that the biblical approach was too simplistic and decided to follow the twelve-step model. We tried to persuade her that only God could set her free and that she would need to depend on Him alone, but she ignored our advice. She started a twelve-step group in her city and is apparently in the same condition now that she was in years ago. In the meantime, those who have thrown themselves on the mercy of the Lord, have had wonderful results!

There is one other spiritual factor we should mention. You cannot speed God up in His processes, but you can do much to slow Him down. In other words, if a woman resists the process the Lord is attempting to lead her through, she is only going to prolong her growth. But as she cooperates, she allows the Holy Spirit full rein to accomplish His marvelous work within her. The Old Testament picture of this is the Israelites who were set free from Egypt. Part of God's plan was to teach them to trust Him before He took them into the Promised Land. This could have been accomplished in a few months, but because of disobedience, they were forced to remain in the wilderness forty years. You cannot hurry God's processes, but you can certainly slow them down.

Overcoming the Mountain

Climbing the steep, rugged mountain to freedom will take time but perseverance and determination will pay off!

Some experience liberty as soon as they have a structured way out. However, most addicts require more time, but as they battle through, the periods of sexual purity will become longer and longer. This was the case in my (Steve) life. I have not met many people during my years of ministry who were more obsessed and out of control with sexual activity than I was. I had gotten to where I was utterly given over to sexual gratification. My battle out of that pit was not an easy struggle. Nevertheless, I was determined to be set free. At first, the addiction seemed like a treacherous mountain climb. As I look back on the process I went through, I now realize that the biblical steps outlined in this book were a stairway leading directly up the side of that mountain.

Yes, an enormous pinnacle loomed high above me. Of course, it was much too high for me to simply jump over. Without a doubt, the more I looked at it, the more impossible it seemed to scale. How did I do it then? I simply took one step at a time. Each day I awoke and purposed to do my best. If I missed the mark, it simply meant that I slipped back a few steps. Before long, I was back to that place on the stairway headed in the upward direction. All I needed to do was keep my eyes on the foothold ahead of me, forgetting how high that mountain was, and continue my ascent, upward bound.

It was not long before I was able to look back and see that I had come a long way. Although I might have still slipped occasionally, I was closer to the Lord than I had ever been and the slips were less frequent. Yes, I had made considerable progress. Somehow, when I considered how far I had come, the distance I had ahead of me no longer seemed like an impossibility. I began to hope.

Eventually, after relentlessly continuing my pursuit of higher elevations and daily adhering to the steps outlined later in this book, my saying "no" to temptation became easier and more automatic in some instances. "No, I don't really *want* to look at porn today!" My personal victories were now outnumbering defeats.

Once, I went several months, only to find myself back into my sin again in early 1985. I had learned to live without illicit sex but had gotten caught on a particularly "weak" day and succumbed to temptation. What followed were a few weeks of major struggling. It proved to be my last fling, however. When I turned away that time, it was for good. Although I would still have occasional struggles after that, the sin had lost its hold on me.

I had climbed up the side of that mountain and did not even know it. It took several months of living a pure life to realize that sexual addiction no longer had a hold on me. I had been so focused on the steps in front of me, that I had forgotten to look at the top of the mountain. It was no longer there! It was behind me!

I wonder what would have happened to me without the steps outlined in this book. I probably would have remained at the bottom, looking up in dismay. I would have been wishing I could be over the top of that mountain, but not knowing quite how to do it. Oh, I would have made an occasional attempt to scale up the side; but without clear direction, it would have simply been a futile endeavor. I would have wandered aimlessly along the side of the hill, not knowing which way to go, and not having anything to cling to. I could have always made a run up the side, full of determination and great effort. Nevertheless, I would have soon tired and fallen back down the hill, more exhausted and discouraged than ever.

I can testify that the only way over that mountain is simply to climb painstakingly upward, a few feet at a time, one day at a time—always moving forward, keeping your eyes on God, and doing your best each day. Unless God chooses to perform some other miracle, this is the only way to get over that mountain.

Dealing With Failures and Guilt

Again, overcoming an enormous mountain like habitual sexual sin usually does not occur quickly. As the woman is in the struggle to overcome, she will have to accept the fact that she may occasionally slip—accept it without using it as an excuse for sin! Each time you give over to sin, you pull yourself further away from God. You will endure additional pain and anguish to make up for lost ground. Please realize and understand that there is a price to pay for failure. This is needful, though. Every failure will only intensify your hatred of the sin. If and when you do fail, it is important not to panic and give up.

Someone said that failure is not falling down; it is remaining there when you have fallen. That is so true! Maybe as you read this book, you are ready to step right into victory—leaving the habit of sin behind you once and for all. Or, it is possible that you may still have a few more slips along the way. God's grace makes provision for slips when a person is sincerely battling. The important thing is to get back up again and resume the fight.

When it comes to one's sense of guilt over sin, it is important to maintain a properly balanced, biblical perspective. If a woman does not experience any sense of guilt, she will never feel compelled to change. On the other hand, if she becomes overwhelmed with guilt, she may lose hope and throw up her hands in defeat. Guilt is a feeling put into our consciences for a good reason. Without experiencing feelings of guilt when we do wrong, we would never be convicted, and thus never know the difference between right and wrong. Guiltiness over sin is a natural response to it.

But God has made provision for our "missing the mark." All we need do is confess the wrongness of our actions to God, asking Him to forgive us, and it is immediately forgotten forever. The Bible says: "If we confess our sins, He is faithful and righteous to forgive us our sins and to cleanse us from all unrighteousness." (I John 1:9) "As far as the east is from the west, so far has He removed our transgressions from us." (Psalm 103:12) "There is therefore now no condemnation for those who are in Christ Jesus." (Romans 8:1)

As we go through this process of coming into freedom, let us keep our eyes on the Lord, not on the sin. If we are always focused on how badly we are doing or our past sinful behavior, we will never sense any victory. As we will discover later in the book, God's grace has the power to take us through this process and to bring us out the other side free of the hold of sin.

*"Yet even now," declares the LORD,
"Return to Me with all your heart, and with
fasting, weeping, and mourning; and rend your
heart and not your garments." (Joel 2:12)*

How badly do you want to be changed? Are you desperate enough to do whatever it takes to be loosed from the ties that bind? Much of the remainder of this book will offer practical steps and techniques that you will need to utilize as you begin your life as an overcoming Christian. True freedom will not come if you do not heed to the biblical approach provided. It is as simple as that.

In the Scripture above, the Lord is compelling His people through the prophet Joel to turn to Him with all their hearts. He knew that half-hearted commitments were not enough. If your problem at all resembles what mine (Steve) was like, you have, no doubt, been lukewarm or even rebellious for years. I was torn between wanting to be a happily married Christian man and still wanting to be a "swinging single." Even after my conversion to Christ, which was a very real experience, I continued to resist doing those things necessary to bring about my deliverance from sexual sin. My faith in Him was so tiny that I lacked the conviction that obeying Him would really bring about results.

Of course, you have a tremendous advantage over me.

I learned these steps the hard way. If I had had the specific guidelines outlined in this book, the length of time it took to overcome my sinful ways of living could have been shortened dramatically. I did not know if I would ever change! I knew of no one with the same problem who had succeeded in overcoming it. You not only have my testimony of victory but the testimonies of hundreds of others whom we have witnessed find freedom through God. This alone should provide a great deal of hope and encouragement to you. You *can* be set free from your bondage. We are not claiming that it will be easy, but you can change if you are willing to follow the steps outlined in this book.

You have probably been agonizing spiritually for months now, complaining bitterly to God about your tormented life. As mentioned before, you cannot blame God for the poor choices you have made. However, He will change you if that is what you sincerely desire. If you really want Him to…it all depends upon your willingness to allow Him to straighten out your crooked path. You may have blamed others for your problems for years, but now it is time to get tough and be determined to beat this thing with the strength and power of God! No one else can do it for you.

What comes to mind is the picture of a boxer who is being pummeled in the corner by the other fighter, when suddenly, he has had enough and comes out swinging! This must also happen to you. You must shake off that complacency and come out swinging! Is this not what the Lord was saying through the prophet Joel: Turn, fast, weep, mourn and rend? These are action words which describe someone determined to get what she needs from the Lord. Winning this battle will require this kind of serious commitment. How can one know that she will truly find freedom from sexual sin by doing these things? The divine "If-Then Principle," as we call it, promises that she will.

The If-Then Principle

Throughout the Bible, God has made a multitude of promises to His people. Many of these promises, however, depend upon the believer doing something first. Although not all of them actually have the words "if-then" contained in them, they all have a conditional nature which is understood. Read each of the following verses as if God were talking directly to you:

> If my people, which are called by my name, shall humble themselves, and pray, and seek my face, and turn from their wicked ways; then will I hear from heaven, and will forgive their sin, and will heal their land. (II Chronicles 7:14)

> Delight yourself in the LORD; and He will give you the desires of your heart. Commit your way to the LORD, trust also in Him, and He will do it. (Psalm 37:4-5)

> Trust in the LORD with all your heart, and do not lean on your own understanding. In all your ways acknowledge Him, and He will make your paths straight. (Proverbs 3:5-6)

> Rejoice in the Lord always; again I will say, rejoice! Let your forbearing spirit be known to all men. The Lord is near. Be anxious for nothing, but in everything by prayer and supplication with thanksgiving let your requests be made known to God. And the peace of God, which surpasses all comprehension, shall guard your hearts and your minds in Christ Jesus. (Philippians 4:4-7)

There is a common theme through all of these promise

verses. *If* we *do* something, i.e. repent, trust, delight, pray, and so on, *then* God will in turn do something for us. Sexual sin is not going to be overcome by sitting back and waiting for God to throw a thunderbolt. The determined woman must initiate the fight herself. Perhaps that's what Jesus meant when He said, "...the kingdom of heaven suffers violence, and violent men take it by force." (Matthew 11:12)

Sometimes we have to do what we know to be right in spite of our feelings. When Steve and I were first married, I worked for awhile in a sweatshop making minimum wage. It was a very dismal workplace. I wanted out of there badly but could not seem to get hired anywhere else. One day, God revealed to Steve that my bad attitude about the place was the hindrance. I would often go in to work late, do a lousy job while I was there, and frequently find some excuse to leave early. Steve told me that God was never going to move me from that job until I changed my attitude. I knew that it was true and determined within myself to be the best employee there. I began going to work on time and putting out more work than ever before. Within *one week* a large insurance company that I had applied at months before hired me!

I learned a valuable lesson from this experience. I could have continued to complain and be ungrateful, but I chose to do what the Lord would have me to do, regardless of the circumstances. God honored that commitment and blessed me greatly. As you look at your circumstances, you must decide if you are going to continue on the easy path, or travel the road the Lord has paved for you. It will not be easy but the "If-Then Principle" promises that He will honor your first step and will help you through this struggle.

Crying Out to God

It is important to understand that God loves His people tremendously and is truly in a passion to help them. When a woman gets to the point of desperately wanting the Lord to remove the sin in her life, she will start crying out to Him for His help, which is never far away. God guarantees freedom to His children, but it is their responsibility to meet the conditions. The "If-Then Principle" helps struggling saints to recognize that if they will cry out for His help without ceasing, He will respond to their appeals. Persistence in prayer was established by God as the means to receiving His help. To further explain this truth, Jesus gave the following two stories which demonstrate the benefit of being bold:

> And He said to them, "Suppose one of you shall have a friend, and shall go to him at midnight, and say to him, 'Friend, lend me three loaves; for a friend of mine has come to me from a journey, and I have nothing to set before him;' and from inside he shall answer and say, 'Do not bother me; the door has already been shut and my children and I are in bed; I cannot get up and give you anything.' I tell you, even though he will not get up and give him anything because he is his friend, yet because of his persistence he will get up and give him as much as he needs." (Luke 11:5-8)

> Now He was telling them a parable to show that at all times they ought to pray and not to lose heart, saying, "There was in a certain city a judge who did not fear God, and did not respect man. And there was a widow in that city, and she kept coming to him, saying, 'Give me legal protection from my opponent.' And for a while he was unwilling; but afterward he said to himself, 'Even though I do not fear God nor respect man, yet because this widow bothers me, I will give her legal protection, lest by continually coming she wear me out.'" And the Lord said, "Hear what the unrighteous judge said; now

shall not God bring about justice for His elect, who
cry to Him day and night, and will He delay long over
them?" (Luke 18:1-7)

No one understands to the fullest all that is involved in
answered prayer or being set free from bondage. However, we
do know that the Lord has given us important principles here
that we can depend on to help us. If you doubt that God really
listens to the cries of His children, examine these passages that
boast of His mercy:

> Then we cried to the LORD, the God of our fathers,
> and the LORD heard our voice and saw our affliction
> and our toil and our oppression; and the LORD brought
> us out of Egypt with a mighty hand and an outstretched
> arm and with great terror and with signs and wonders;
> (Deuteronomy 26:7-8)

> And when the sons of Israel cried to the LORD,
> the LORD raised up a deliverer for the sons of Israel to
> deliver them, Othniel the son of Kenaz, Caleb's younger
> brother. (Judges 3:9)

> But when the sons of Israel cried to the LORD, the
> LORD raised up a deliverer for them, Ehud the son of
> Gera, the Benjamite, a left-handed man. (Judges 3:15)

> And the sons of Israel cried to the LORD…And
> the LORD routed Sisera and all his chariots and all his
> army, with the edge of the sword before Barak; and
> Sisera alighted from his chariot and fled away on foot.
> (Judges 4:3, 15)

> Now it came about when the sons of Israel cried to

the LORD on account of Midian, that the LORD sent
a prophet to the sons of Israel. (Judges 6:7-8)

These passages are just a few accounts of God's response
to the cries of His people. Time and time again the nation
of Israel would get themselves into trouble because of their
disobedience. Yet, whenever they cried out to God for His help,
He would rescue them. Your situation might be much the same
as that of Israel. It is because of your disobedience that you
are in the predicament you find yourself in, and yet there is a
merciful God who hears the cries of His children.

I (Steve) once thought that all of the trips I made to the
altar crying out for God's help were a waste of time. Then as
I re-examined those isolated incidents, I came to realize that
those trips to the altar were instrumental in bringing about my
deliverance. If you really want to be set free from the bondage
of sexual sin, cry out to God daily. Do it today! Do it now! Your
cries will be heard!

The Prayer of Faith

There is one more aspect to the cry for help which is
very important. The prayer of faith plays a major role in the
struggling Christian's ultimate deliverance. In spite of what
some teach, faith is not something that is simply mustered up
through the denial of reality (e.g. the sick person who denies
the sickness is there, etc.). The center of the Christian faith is
Christ, and our faith is inextricably tied to who He is. What a
woman believes about the Lord determines everything in her
life as a believer. Thus, for the most part, our ability to believe
the Lord for victory is directly determined by our level of
trust in Him. This trust is based in one's knowledge of His
character. God is ever at work attempting to instill a sense of
His trustworthiness to His children. Those who come into a

closer, more intimate relationship with the Lord find Him to be a sweet, loving Person.

One of the terrible and frightening aspects of sin is the unbelief that it fosters. The more deeply entrenched the sin, the greater the darkness of unbelief. Many men who come to the Pure Life Ministries live-in program are very cynical. Part of the problem, of course, is that they have heard countless empty promises touted by those trying to draw followers to their particular system of recovery. We are not overly concerned when a man arrives with a skeptical attitude because we know that within a month or so he will see the reality of God, which will provoke a great deal of hope within him.

However, there are always those who will not believe the best about God. They are like the wicked servant Jesus spoke of who attempted to justify his irresponsibility by redirecting the blame at God: "'Master, I knew you to be a hard man.'" (Matthew 25:24) Many choose to believe God is harsh in order to somehow justify their disobedience. As was the case with the servant who hid his talent, excuses will not alter the course of reality on the day of reckoning.

The fact is, the Lord greatly desires to help the struggling believer and is available to provide the necessary power to overcome if the woman will only humble herself and ask. The believing prayer says, "Lord, I realize that it is my fault that I am in this predicament. I come to Your throne looking for mercy. My request is not based on any merit of my own, but upon Your great heart. I believe what the Bible says about You. You are a God of mercy and compassion, and I believe that You will help me out of this mess because of what You are like." This is the prayer which the Lord will be quick to answer.

CREATE IN ME A PURE HEART

Part 3: INFLUENCES

CHAPTER TEN:
THE SINFUL FLESH

"Now the deeds of the flesh are evident, which are:
immorality, impurity, sensuality, idolatry. . . ."
(Galatians 5:19-20)

In the next three chapters, we will examine the three forces which work tirelessly to compel us toward sin. They are the flesh, the world, and the enemy.

Let us first explore "the flesh," which is the only influence, of the three, generated from ourselves. The Bible primarily utilizes this term as a designation of mankind. Genesis 6:12 is one example: "And God looked on the earth, and behold, it was corrupt; for all flesh had corrupted their way upon the earth." Man's primary composition is flesh and so the term is used representatively of people throughout the Scriptures. Even in the spiritual sense, a person is confined to his or her fleshly body with the soul and spirit residing within it simultaneously. Where the woman's body is, she is. Whatever happens to the body, befalls the woman. Until her physical death, her soul accompanies her body. It is the body of a person which we see and interact with.

The Physical Drive

Human beings were created with certain innate drives, impulses, and appetites such as hunger, thirst, and even the desire for sex. There is nothing wrong with sex as long as it is confined to intimacy between a man and his wife. God wants married couples, whom He has enjoined, to enjoy each other—thus, He made sex a pleasurable experience. However, confusion and perversion emerge when people deviate from the purpose for which God ordained sex.

The desire for sex is one of the basic, physical drives of the human being. It is among hunger, thirst, and sleep as the most important natural impulses. God instilled these desires in us, and designed them to be enjoyable experiences, so that we would do the things required to exist and survive as individual people and as a species. If we did not have hunger, how often would we eat? If we did not experience thirst, how often would we drink? If we did not grow sleepy, when would our bodies get rest? If God had not put a wholesome desire within us to have sex, how would we reproduce?

As with all of these drives, when someone abuses the purpose for sex, it becomes doubly hard to get it back under control. A woman who has become addicted to alcohol or drugs has a tremendous battle in order to break free. Her freedom from their grim pull depends largely upon her willingness to modify certain aspects of her lifestyle, i.e. old acquaintances, certain neighborhoods, etc.

However, for the one who is addicted to food or sex, such modifications will only benefit her to a certain degree. She will always be around food and people at some point in her life and be forced to deal with an inbred desire for food or sex—these desires are virtually impossible to avoid. An alcoholic could go through her entire life without ever handling another drink, but a woman given over to sexual sin must learn to control her appetites. This is an extremely difficult thing to do; hence, it is not easy for the addict to escape the bondage of sexual sin. In addition to the incessant cries and ruthless demands of her flesh for more, she has the world constantly telling her that she can have more any time, any place, and with whomever she desires.

The Flesh Nature

The term *flesh* in the New Testament means something more than simply mankind in general, the meat on a person's bones or even the basic animal drives that compel a person to eat and drink. One Bible dictionary defines it as, "…the natural man, including the unrenewed will and mind, moving in the world of self and sense only."[1] As such, the flesh has a natural opposition to the demands of the Holy Spirit.

In two distinct passages, the Apostle Paul touches on some of the aspects of the flesh:

> For those who are according to the flesh set their minds on the things of the flesh, but those who are according to the Spirit, the things of the Spirit. For the mind set on the flesh is death, but the mind set on the Spirit is life and peace, because the mind set on the flesh is hostile toward God; for it does not subject itself to the law of God, for it is not even able to do so; and those who are in the flesh cannot please God…if you are living according to the flesh, you must die; but if by the Spirit you are putting to death the deeds of the body, you will live. (Romans 8:5-8, 13)

> But I say, walk by the Spirit, and you will not carry out the desire of the flesh. For the flesh sets its desire against the Spirit, and the Spirit against the flesh; for these are in opposition to one another, so that you may not do the things that you please…Now the deeds of the flesh are evident, which are: immorality, impurity, sensuality, idolatry, sorcery, enmities, strife, jealousy, outbursts of anger, disputes, dissensions, factions,

envying, drunkenness, carousing, and things like these, of which I forewarn you, just as I have forewarned you, that those who practice such things will not inherit the kingdom of God. (Galatians 5:16-21)

We will discuss the battle between the Spirit and flesh in greater detail later. For now, we need to see the character of the fallen nature as it stands in contrast to the Spirit. In short, the flesh desires only that which brings it gratification. It is selfish and the more one indulges its desires, the more self-centered one will become.

Sin is another factor to be considered. A person's physical nature is not concerned with pleasing God. It is only interested in comfort, pleasure, and the preservation of self. The flesh longs for gratification at any cost. It always seeks that which is sensual and satisfying. God, family and others take a secondary position to personal interests. It only wants its lusts and desires to be fully satisfied.

Before a woman comes to Christ, she lives her life completely under the auspices of her demanding flesh.* The unquenchable desires of the flesh ultimately drive her to do things which are in total opposition to the nature and kingdom of God. Sin acts as the ruling influence within the woman's being. Indeed, every human being is born with a corrupted nature bent toward sin.

Living under the dominion of a sinful nature establishes habits which eventually form a lifestyle. Deep ruts are dug into the woman's life through repeated behavior. She becomes comfortable responding to her inner longings. Typically, by the time she becomes a believer, the passions of the flesh have already ruled her life for many years. These deeply entrenched

---

* This explains the biblical connection between the lust of the flesh and the world. (cf. I John 2:16; II Peter 1:4; etc.) The world consists of the unregenerated masses of mankind who live out their lives dominated by "the lust of the flesh."

habits have been constantly reinforced and strengthened by the old nature which has become accustomed to having its own way. When the desire for sexual behavior wells up within her, she gives into the craving without a second thought. Again, the foundational purpose for life, even for the most decent nonbeliever, revolves around pleasure, gratification, and self-preservation.

The Inner Man

Scripture employs various words to describe the inner man: *heart, soul, mind, spirit, inward parts*, etc. Although they are often used interchangeably, when studying these biblical terms in depth, a definable quality of each emerges.

The soul seems to be the term that most comprehensively describes the inner man. The word *soul* (Hb. *nephesh*; Gk. *psuche*) is primarily used to designate someone's physical life (Matthew 2:20) and individuality (II Peter 2:14) in conjunction with the unseen part of a person that continues on into the realm of eternity after the physical body has died. (Genesis 35:18)

In three succinct statements, Jesus shows the eternal nature of the soul, along with the terrible implications of neglecting it: "This very night your soul is required of you." (Luke 12:20) "For what will a man be profited, if he gains the whole world, and forfeits his soul?" (Matthew 16:26) "...fear Him who is able to destroy both soul and body in hell." (Matthew 10:28)

As has been mentioned, the soul houses the entire inner life of a human being. Within the soul is an integrated system of various components which work together in much the same way as one's internal organs. At the expense of oversimplifying this complex spiritual organism (with its often overlapping parts), I would divide the inner man into two basic components: mind and heart. The human spirit, as will be seen later, seems to be located in the innermost part of a person's heart.

Soul

Mind	Heart
Thinking	Personality
Intellect	Emotions
Reason	Feelings
Perception	Motives
Imagination	Attitudes
Memory	Character
Wit	Values
Decision-making	Will
Evaluation	Conscience
	Spirit

If one were to compare a person's inner workings to a computer, the heart would be the memory, the keyboard would be the senses that bring information into the computer, and the central processing unit would be the mind which completes all of the functions.

The mind is the functioning agent of consciousness that allows the human to think, reason, comprehend, perceive and consider things. People use their minds to contemplate profound subjects, envision great enterprises, and imagine a wide variety of ideas. Some people have extremely strong memories, capable of recalling obsolete numbers on a moment's notice or memorizing Scripture by the chapter. Others possess a quick wit, able to instantly make funny statements. Still others are deeply intellectual, possessing the mental capacity to think through complicated problems until they have arrived at the correct solution. The mind contains the mysterious interface between the physiological (our brain) and the spiritual (our soul).

The human mind regularly receives visits from random thoughts, memories, and ideas that seem to drift in like so much flotsam. Also coming and going are emotional impulses, vague feelings and arousing sensations. Beyond all of these are the wide variety of outside stimuli that enters this interior realm through the five senses (touch, taste, see, hear and smell). And, of course, we have an enemy who is able to introduce thoughts that tempt one to sin.

More than anything, the human mind is a working machine that sifts through this enormous amount of data to make decisions by the thousands on a daily basis. And it is this aspect of the mind that, at least spiritually speaking, is the most important. For the choices humans make determine actions, which, in turn, establish behavior patterns, which ultimately determine a person's destiny.

However, it should be noted that many times people sin without purposing to sin. Our fallen natures are so bent toward sin that we can naturally indulge sinful thoughts without even trying. One person defined the flesh as, "the inward principle of evil which possesses our nature, and lies back of the will, beyond the reach of our power..."[2] This explains why counselees have sometimes told us, "I found myself fantasizing about that person." That comes about because the human mind, like the computer that continues its functions even when the operator is not directing it, also has an automatic mode. The "default" mindset of human beings is always bent toward fulfilling the desires of the flesh. Thus, a woman can come to her senses, realizing she has been indulging in sexual fantasy without intending to do so.

The Indwelling Spirit

In our feeble attempt to describe the intricacies of the inner man, we placed the mind and heart side-by-side in their relationship to each other within the human soul. In reality, a deep well would be a more fitting picture. (Psalm 64:6) At the top of this well is the conscious activity of the mind. Down one level, would be the different faculties which the mind can draw from: the memory, imagination, etc. Go a little deeper and you come to the human emotions with all of their fickle desires and fluctuating feelings. Descend still further and you come to the will, where life's decisions are made.

At the very bottom, deep within the human heart, is what we would term a spiritual womb. It is here, through the repentance of sin and putting one's faith in Christ, that a person may receive the "incorruptible" seed of the Living God. In much the same fashion that the Holy Spirit "came upon" and "overshadowed" Mary, Christ's mother, so too does this divine Visitor come to the human being whose heart has opened up to receive Him. (Acts 16:14) This is the new birth of which Jesus spoke. (John 3:3-8) Paul said, "Do you not know that you are a temple of God and *that* the Spirit of God dwells in you?" (I Corinthians 3:16) It is the human spirit that receives this heavenly Guest to enter and dwell within the person.

This mystical union of God's Spirit and man's spirit creates new life within the person. When the Spirit of God resides within a person, everything is changed. Whereas before, most decisions of life were made with the intention of satisfying his or her natural desires, now the person is imparted with a whole new value system. Though a new morality has been infused into the person, the physical longings of the flesh are still relentless in exerting their influence. Thus, we find Paul agonizing over the age-old struggle of believers: "For the flesh sets its desire against the Spirit, and the Spirit against the flesh; for these are in opposition to one another, so that you may not do the things that you please." (Galatians 5:17) Elsewhere Paul writes: "For I know that nothing good dwells in me, that is, in my flesh; for the willing is present in me, but the doing of the good *is* not. For the good that I want, I do not do, but I practice the very evil that I do not want." (Romans 7:18-19) There is now a war that takes place within the person that was nonexistent before.

There was no battle previously because the flesh enjoyed total freedom in having its way.

It is significant to note that Jesus described the conversion experience as being "born again." In fact, much of the New Testament describes a process of growth whereby those who are "babes in Christ" gradually reach spiritual maturity. Unfortunately, many Christians remain immature for a time. However, if they have truly been born again, they will not remain that way. The Spirit of Christ dwelling within them will be constantly prodding them toward the things of God.

Nevertheless, when the person first surrenders to Christ, the flesh is a powerful, muscular force. Comparatively, the spirit is an underfed weakling! However, as the Christian begins to mature spiritually, the spirit becomes stronger and more able to subdue the flesh as God intended.

Be that as it may, our entire time on this earth will be characterized by the internal battle between the flesh and Spirit. Although it is our spirit that fights for godliness, it is our will that ultimately makes the final decision. God gave every person a free will to choose between right and wrong. Every moment we must decide which side we will feed. Just as the flesh grows stronger when we feed it with sensuous living, our spirit grows stronger when it is nourished with the things of God. Paul said it this way: "…for whatever a man sows, this he will also reap. For the one who sows to his own flesh shall from the flesh reap corruption, but the one who sows to the Spirit shall from the Spirit reap eternal life." (Galatians 6:8)

Which will you feed the most? Will you feed your carnal nature, building it stronger and stronger? Or will you strengthen your spiritual nature? Paul strongly exhorts us: "But put on the Lord Jesus Christ, and make no provision for the flesh in regard to *its* lusts." (Romans 13:14) The remainder of this book will teach you how to methodically put on the Lord Jesus Christ, as well as how to quit providing sustenance for your flesh. As the spirit in you is nurtured, strengthened, and renewed, the old, carnal nature *will* gradually weaken and wither.

The Power of Habit

Many people encounter difficulty overcoming the power of the flesh because they have spent many years developing specific patterns of life which are hard to modify. A lifestyle is made up of various habits. Abandoning a life catered to the flesh in order to obtain one controlled by the Spirit requires changing certain routines. The late Nelson E. Hinman discusses the "Power of Habit:"

> But I say the power of habit is rooted in the deepest recesses of our minds, well below the areas of quick recall…All of our skills are developed by good practiced habits. It gets down into our subconscious mind and controls us. As long as you drive your car having to think about everything you do, you are a dangerous driver. But by "practicing" your driving, it becomes *habit*. Once you establish the habit of driving, you become a very good driver. How do you do this? By practice…
>
> The thing we don't realize is that by the same way we can develop bad habits. Baseball players sometimes develop bad habits. That is what coaches are for; they spot a player who is developing a bad habit and they work with them until they eliminate it. You can understand that but the thing you probably do not stop to think about is that by this same identical process we develop emotional habits; both good and bad…
>
> We can understand this a little more clearly if we talk about anger. Anger is a learned response. I know, for I had a problem with anger for over twenty years…I got that way by habitual response. I learned to do it. The

more I practiced at it the better I got at it. Well, I had to learn how to reverse it...

We can train our minds to act any way we want them to act, up to a given point. But there is a thing in the Bible called "sin" that interrupts the best you can do. However, it is not placed beyond your control because God has given us a book of directions and instructions on how to deal with those things.[3]

People bound up in sexual sin have developed habits of responding sexually to outside stimuli. Over the years they have learned to react to certain situations with lust or fantasy. When I (Steve) would drive down the street and see a pretty girl walking, I would leer at her. This eventually became a habit. When I used to go to bed with my wife, I often fantasized about other women. When I felt the urge for illicit sex, I was accustomed to yielding without a fight. I needed to learn to break these awful habits and exercise self-control. How? By practice!

Practice Makes Perfect

Paul and Peter both understood the importance of establishing proper habits through practice.

Finally, brethren, whatever is true, whatever is honorable, whatever is right, whatever is pure, whatever is lovely, whatever is of good repute, if there is any excellence and if anything worthy of praise, let your mind dwell on these things. The things you have learned and received and heard and seen in me, *practice* these things; and the God of peace shall be with you. (Philippians 4:8-9)

For by these He has granted to us His precious and

magnificent promises, in order that by them you might become partakers of the divine nature, having escaped the corruption that is in the world by lust.

Now for this very reason also, applying all diligence, in your faith supply moral excellence, and in your moral excellence, knowledge; and in your knowledge, self-control, and in your self-control, perseverance, and in your perseverance, godliness; and in your godliness, brotherly kindness, and in your brotherly kindness, love...

Therefore, brethren, be all the more diligent to make certain about His calling and choosing you; for as long as you *practice* these things, you will never stumble. (II Peter 1:4-7, 10)

We can see in these two sections of Scripture that we have a choice about what we *practice*. If we practice (or sow) ungodliness, then we will desire (or reap) more ungodliness. By the same token, if we practice godliness, then we will desire a greater godliness. Feelings always follow behavior. The proper habits need to be established into our minds, and as they are, we will *desire* to continue in them.

The primary enemy we will face is our own fallen nature. It is our flesh that longs for gratification. It is within these recesses that sin abides. Although we are under an attack from without, if we can win the war within, the outside enemies will fall before us. This is one of the most important secrets to breaking free from sexual bondage.

CHAPTER ELEVEN:
SEPARATING FROM THE WORLD

*"Enter by the narrow gate; for the gate is wide, and
the way is broad that leads to destruction,
and many are those who enter by it." (Matthew 7:13)*

It is easy to understand why people in this day and age have a
misconception about sex. Everywhere one turns, she finds the
promotion and exploitation of sex. Hollywood is committed
to portraying the hero as the master seducer. Movies are overrun
with beautiful, scantily clad (or nude) starlets. Advertisers blatantly
use sex to sell their products. Fashion designers do their utmost to
make sure that young women show off as much flesh as possible.
Company parties hire male or female strippers for entertainment.
Homosexuality is unashamedly flaunted and advocated. People
openly live together in sin. Needless to say, the moral fabric of
our society is being unraveled right before our eyes.

Society teaches young people that illicit sex is not only
accepted, but expected. Take the daily life of an average
fourteen-year old girl. While she's waiting for her younger sister
to get ready for school, she turns on MTV and catches some of
the latest videos, most of them filled with plenty of innuendo
and skin. Later that morning her health class teacher refuses to
take a moral stand against pre-marital sex or even homosexuality,
and a text message from the cute guy at school invites her out
on a date. While she walks down the hallway she overhears the

popular girls talking about their sexual escapades.

On the way home from school, she stops at a friend's house to login to their MySpace.com accounts and cruise the latest pix and posts from their "friends," hoping some of the guys they are looking to hook up with have responded. A few hours later, she is home and in front of the TV, where the characters of her favorite shows regularly engage in various sexual scenarios. Her favorite starlet is almost always hooking up with someone. Then there are the commercials that showcase beautiful women selling anything and everything imaginable. *Cosmo Girl* and *Seventeen* magazines are laden with seductive advertisements and answers to the latest questions about sex posted by the readers.

With such overwhelming exposure as this, why should anyone be surprised that a young teenager indulges in sex? Especially considering that "teens spend an average of four to six hours per day interacting with the mass media in various forms."[1]

A permissive society, such as ours, makes the road to habitual sexual sin very smooth. Just as our culture makes it easy for a woman to slide down the path deeper and deeper into bondage, it also makes it equally difficult for the woman, who so desires, to escape it. Everywhere she turns, she is constantly confronted with and reminded of what she is trying to avoid. Erwin Lutzer gives his viewpoint of society's reasoning: "For those who believe in free love, sex is primarily a physical experience. When you're hungry you eat, when you're tired you sleep, and when you're turned on, you have sex. Such reasoning may sound right, but it's off the target by a mile."[2] Lester Sumrall says, "The carnal world would have us believe that pleasure is the only purpose of sex. Some prudish Christians think that pleasure has nothing to do with sex. Both are wrong."[3]

Consequently, when a woman grows up in a society that presents this hedonistic message, which is basically: "If it feels good, just do it," it is very hard for her mind to dismiss the untruth of it. If she becomes born-again, she suddenly finds herself striving against the powerful flow of this world, with all of its seductive charms. She must take a stand for righteousness, although everything in her carnal nature longs for what the world offers.

Separating Ourselves

Paul, as he was trying to encourage the believers who lived in the immoral climate of Corinth, said the following:

> Do not be bound together with unbelievers; for what partnership have righteousness and lawlessness, or what fellowship has light with darkness? Or what harmony has Christ with Belial, or what has a believer in common with an unbeliever? Or what agreement has the temple of God with idols? For we are the temple of the living God; just as God said, "I will dwell in them and walk among them; and I will be their God, and they shall be My people. Therefore, come out from their midst and be separate," says the Lord. "And do not touch what is unclean; and I will welcome you. And I will be a father to you, and you shall be sons and daughters to Me," says the Lord Almighty. (II Corinthians 6:14-18)

God has called us to *separate* ourselves from the world. Saints down through the ages have understood the necessity of turning their backs on the world and its immoral value system if they were to experience a vibrant walk with God. Enoch, Noah, Abraham, Moses, the Prophets, John the Baptist and the Apostles all lived this way; not to mention the majority of Christians down through the ages. What Jesus said has always been true, "No one can serve two masters; for either he will hate the one and love the other, or he will hold to the one and despise the other. You cannot serve God *and* Mammon."

(Matthew 6:24) Those who endeavor to escape the pollutions of this world will only be able to do so as they sever themselves from its corrupting influences.

But in America, the majority of Evangelicals have glossed over this inescapable and essential truth. They want to have both, and have, by and large, created a culture and gospel that allows them to live for the "passing pleasures" of Egypt (Hebrews 11:25) and still claim heaven as their eternal home. A. W. Tozer explained it this way: "Men think of the world, not as a battleground but as a playground. We are not here to fight, we are here to frolic. We are not in a foreign land, we are at home. We are not getting ready to live, we are already living, and the best we can do is rid ourselves of our inhibitions and our frustrations and live this life to the full."[4] How could we ever hope to cleanse our minds from the filth of our past if we continue to wallow in the world's sensuous thinking?

Americans First

As saints (literally *called out ones*) we are to live as "strangers and pilgrims on the earth." (Hebrews 11:13 KJV) We are to "keep seeking the things above" (Colossians 3:1), "for our citizenship is in heaven, from which also we eagerly wait for a Savior, the Lord Jesus Christ." (Philippians 3:20) True conversion results in a translation from the "domain of darkness" into the "kingdom of His beloved Son." (Colossians 1:13) When a woman is saved, she is saved *out of* the dominion of darkness and *into* the dominion of Light. And "what fellowship has light with darkness?" (II Corinthians 6:14)

Paul told the Ephesians, "you were formerly darkness, but now you are light in the Lord; *walk as children of light.*" (Ephesians 5:8, emphasis added) Our distinction in the world is supposed to be that we are light, which is frequently contrasted in the Bible with "the darkness of this world." (Ephesians 6:12 KJV) So why then does the lifestyle of the average American Christian offer little, if any, distinction from the lifestyle of the rest of the American population? If one is light and the other darkness, why is it nearly impossible to tell them apart?

The answer is a phenomenon that has become a hallmark of the American Evangelical movement: *they are Americans first and Christians second.* American Evangelicals have created a church subculture, and even a gospel, that suits their entertainment-driven and prosperity-laden lifestyles, and in so doing have introduced their own sanctified brand of the American dream. How many Christians that you know live just as much for the weekend as the rest of their unsaved coworkers? How many are just as obsessed with worldly fashion and in just as much debt while endeavoring to fill their houses full of all the same adult toys?

The heart of a person who has grown up in this kind of environment is fertile ground for sexual sin. Consider what the Lord said when He revealed the root of Sodom's sexual sins:

> "Behold, this was the guilt of your sister Sodom: she and her daughters had arrogance, abundant food and careless ease, but she did not help the poor and needy. Thus they were haughty and committed abominations before Me. Therefore I removed them when I saw *it.*" (Ezekiel 16:49-50)

This passage exposes the indulgent lifestyle that precipitated the gross immorality that became their hallmark. Their prosperity allowed them to pursue comfort and pleasure as the overriding concerns of life. Rather than meeting the needs of the poor, they lived for themselves. Eventually sexual sin overran their culture. Does any of this sound familiar?

A Demonic Conspiracy

The enemy has been able to use the technological advances of the past half-century to deepen its grip on the soul of our nation. The various forms of media are utilized to break down godly standards in the Church. Way back in the 1970's David Wilkerson wrote about the effects of television upon the home:

> Satan is succeeding through television in a way not possible by any other kind of demonic invasion. Through that speaking idol, he can accomplish in this generation what he accomplished in Eden…But the sodomites are in now—in our homes. And we are now the blinded ones. Homosexual writers, actors, and producers flaunt their evil right before our eyes; and admit it or not, you and all in your home are under a demonic sodomite attack.[5]

It almost seems as though there is a demonic conspiracy in America to control and utterly possess the minds of Christians.

Since nearly everyone watches television and surfs the Internet, Christians assume it must be acceptable. In fact, television has become such an integral part of the American Christian's life that the woman who does not include it into her life is considered odd or fanatical—*by Christians*! Even family togetherness in many homes is centered around "the tube." God warned the people of Israel against this thinking: "You shall not follow a multitude in doing evil." (Exodus 23:2) Just because it seems everyone indulges in these things does not mean that it is right, nor does it mean that we will not be held accountable for our own choices.

The Effects of Television

Many saints believe they are capable of watching television without being affected by it. It may seem to a woman that she has complete control over what she accepts when she watches television, but that is not the case. Television is geared toward mind control and successfully brainwashes viewers each day. That is the reason advertisers are so willing to pay millions of dollars for a few seconds of advertising time. Dr. Jenson explains the effects of television on the Christian:

> Satan uses the world's system obviously and boldly. He works through our schools, universities, and governments, but most overtly through the media. And the most powerful tool of the media is television. It should be obvious to us today that Satan is using television in a mighty way. We are surrounded by strategic warfare that is calculated to immobilize Christians...
>
> Children basically learn from the time of infancy by seeing, and their emotions are directly connected to these "images" even before they can talk. And adults are not really different. A film or television program often moves directly past our thinking, rational minds to our emotions, apart from any rational, spiritual evaluation...
>
> Harvard University concluded a project which included a comprehensive study on television's role on the sexual education of children. Their study revealed that 70% of all allusions to intercourse on television involve unmarried couples or prostitutes. Much of television's erotic activity involves violence against women, which is reflected in statistics which show that 50% of all women in this country have been victims of rape, incest, or battery...
>
> You might say that this does not affect you or your children because you are a committed Christian. That is just not true. Satan is subtle—he develops attitudes slowly. This is not a crusade against television. I am

just saying that we are experiencing warfare against our minds. The point is that television has desensitized Christians to sin and pain while filling our minds with artificial emotion and unreality. For many children, the test of reality is whether or not they have seen it on television. If they have not, then it is not real...

This subtle brainwashing goes on day after day. The need for solitude and quietness was never greater than it is now.

Satan uses the world's system to stimulate our sin.[6]

The next time you watch television, pay attention to what the commercials say. Notice that they are telling you what to do, as you sit there passively allowing them to do so. "Buy this if you want to be beautiful." "Buy this if you want your house to be the nicest on the block." "Buy this if you want to be accepted by your peers." "Buy this if you want to enjoy yourself." Mind control. It is scary to even think about how much power television has. How does the pleasure-is-everything mindset propagated by television affect a Christian woman's need for inner sobriety? What is the cumulative effect of seeing sexual innuendo night after night on TV? How is she affected when she accumulates countless hours watching situation comedies that mock everything which is decent?

Television can be compared to hypnosis, a tool that is used to put a person in a passive state to accept subconsciously what he or she would not accept under normal consciousness. Television is a lethal weapon that the enemy is using to desensitize, demoralize, and eventually destroy the minds of people. Donald Wildmon is aware of the way it is being used against believers:

Television is the most pervasive and persuasive medium we have. At times it is larger than life. It is our only true national medium. Network television is the greatest educator we have. It tells us, in its programming, what is right and wrong, what is acceptable and unacceptable, whom to believe and not to believe, whom to trust and not trust, and whom we should desire to emulate...

It is teaching that adultery is an acceptable and approved lifestyle. It is teaching that violence is a legitimate way to achieve one's goals or to resolve conflict. It is teaching that profanity is the language of the respectable. But these are only surface messages. The real message is deeper.

It is teaching that hardly anyone goes to church, that very few people in our society are Christian or live by Christian principles. How? By simply censoring Christian characters, Christian values, and Christian culture from the programs. It is teaching that people who claim to be Christian are hypocrites, cheats, liars, or worse. It does so by characterization.[7]

How would you feel if someone put you in front of several thousand people and started ridiculing your belief in God? That is exactly what television is doing. Its producers are laughing at and mocking God's people. Have we become so calloused that we are still willing to align ourselves with the world system which hates the things of God? It is tragic that Christians are so well versed in the most popular situation comedies, the funniest commercials, the hottest dramas, and yet spend such little, precious time quietly before God, studying and meditating on Scripture and interceding for the lost.

Unfortunately, people are quite addicted to television. The question is often raised about what one would do to escape boredom without the TV, as if that somehow justifies the spiritual cost it exacts. We, too, thought this way when we first entered into "life after television." The evening hours seemed to go at a snail's pace those first few weeks. It was not long, however, before those empty hours became filled with meaningful times together and enjoyable times of real fellowship with other believers. It is never easy to break a habit the flesh has become accustomed to, but the grace of God is available for those who are determined to cut themselves off from the influences of this world system.

The Internet and the Rising Tide of Evil

If television broke down the righteous standards of the Church in the latter half of the 20th Century, the Internet has taken it even further. Has any medium of information enslaved more people to evil in as short a time as the World Wide Web? How many of us can even clearly remember what it was like to do our jobs without the use of email and the Internet? Cell phones, iPods, MySpace, the web, chat, email, satellite TV...Information is increasing at exponential levels, just as the prophet Daniel predicted it would. And with that increase in information has come a rising tide of evil that has wreaked more havoc on the Church than we have yet to see manifest itself.

In the late 1990's, who could have predicted what was about to sweep across the world? The click of a computer mouse was about to open an unimaginable Pandora's Box of intense pleasure and evil. By the year 2000, the phrase "Internet porn" began to be a common refrain in pastors' offices across our nation.

The Internet, touted as the benefactor of mankind for the Twenty-first Century, with all its wonderful means of conveying useful information and services to the shrinking global community, also became an abyss of the raunchiest filth and most enticing allurements of sexual imagery ever assembled. While no one was looking, people who would have otherwise never walked into an adult bookstore began filling their minds with image after image of pornography. But not only that, it is one of the vehicles that the devil has constructed to fuse the inhabitants of this world into "one mind" that is saturated with *his* value system, *his* perspectives, what *he* loves and what *he* lives for.

We fear most believers are much too naive when it comes to their perception of the web. As with most things they enjoy, they see in them the good that they want to see; that is how they insulate themselves from suffering the possible loss of them. It is human nature. They see the convenience and the speed with which they can get answers to the questions they have: driving directions to their destination, the weather forecast, news and so on. But what about the times they are so easily enticed into reading something spiritually unedifying? Or how about the hours their kids spend in such virtual worlds as MySpace or Xanga? Do they see how the enemy is shaping their perspectives and values through the corrupting influences of their godless peers? Do they make the connection between their waning hunger for God and the increase in their time spent surfing the web?

While the Internet has many practical and useful applications to their daily lives, believers must see past that which seems innocuous and see that there is a Mastermind that is quietly using such technology to enslave people to a lifestyle driven by and devoted to the spirit of antichrist. How many times have you heard someone say, "How did we ever live without this?" Beware of what lurks just beyond that statement.

The Passivity of the American Church

Given the reality of such a striking comparison between the Sodomite and American cultures, one would think believers in America would be on high alert against the worldly enticements emanating from our culture of abundance. Peter said, "Be sober, be vigilant; because your adversary the devil, as a roaring lion, walketh about, seeking whom he may devour." (I Peter 5:8 KJV) In this brief passage of Scripture, Peter stresses the importance of carefully guarding our minds against the "wiles of the devil."

Be sober and vigilant. These words create an image of a soldier standing on guard duty, expecting to be attacked by enemy forces at any moment—completely alert. There is no time for slumber. He must vigilantly keep watch lest the enemy slips in unawares. How can the enemy do this? Let us take a look at the opposite of vigilance, which is passivity. Webster defines passive as: "Not active, but acted upon; affected by outside force or agency. Receiving or enduring without resistance or emotional reaction; submissive."[8]

This is what has taken place in the majority of the Christian population in America today. We have become so enslaved to maintaining a life of pleasure and comfort that we are spiritually lethargic. Rather than aggressively tearing down the strongholds of the enemy and waging a war for the souls of our loved ones, we have allowed the enemy to ravage, plunder and exploit us. Instead of affecting the world around us for the cause of Christ, we have allowed this world's system to dictate our lives. Consequently, we are spiritually unfit for war; we have become spiritually fat and lazy. Paul said, "Suffer hardship with me, as a good soldier of Christ Jesus. No soldier in active service entangles himself in the affairs of everyday life, so that he may please the one who enlisted him as a soldier." (II Timothy 2:3-4)

The Christian struggling with sexual sin must acquire a new attitude about what Christian living is all about. Our purpose in life is not to greedily fulfill every desire; we are here to serve the One who has called us. We are not to be gluttons for pleasure, but rather soldiers willing to suffer hardship for the sake of Christ. Rather than being immersed in the sensuous living of the world, we should be separated from it. In one poignant statement loaded with meaning for each of our lives, Paul tells us not to "be conformed to this world, but be transformed by the renewing of your mind, that you may prove what the will of God is, that which is good and acceptable and perfect." (Romans 12:2) As we saw earlier, God's will is for His children to be transformed into the likeness of His Son. (Romans 8:29) How does this transformation occur? It happens by a renewal of the mind. The mentality of the world must be put off and replaced with the mind of Christ. As Paul said, "You were taught, with regard to your former way of life, to put off your old self, which is being corrupted by its deceitful desires; to be made new in the attitude of your minds; and to put on the new self, created to be like God in true righteousness and holiness." (Ephesians 4:22-24 NIV)

Being a Christian means to be alive and active. It could be compared to fish. A live and healthy fish is constantly swimming against the current of the river. The easy thing for him to do would be to float along, but he has a natural inclination to fight the current. A dead or sickly fish, on the other hand, puts up little or no struggle. He just floats downstream with all of the other debris and weak ones. Does this at all describe your spiritual life?

Radical Amputation

For many, the decision they make on this particular issue will determine their degree of victory in the future. Those unwilling to cut themselves off from the spirit of this world will find that they have very little strength to take the other necessary steps to overcome the hold of sexual sin on their lives.

We must get brutally honest with ourselves. What is more important to us: living a holy life pleasing to God or indulging ourselves in the entertainment and pleasure of this world? Do you succumb to temptation while you are on the Internet? Jesus said, "…If your right eye causes you to sin, pluck it out." (Matthew 5:29 NKJV) Are you lured into sexual or romantic fantasy by the TV? "Cut it off and throw it away; it is better that you lose one of your members than that your whole body go into hell." (Matthew 5:30 RSV)

For those who have given themselves over to sexual sin, a definite "plucking out" and "cutting off" needs to occur in these areas of their lives. At the very least, the computer should be in a high traffic area of the home and equipped with a good Internet filter. Further, godly accountability and a severe limiting of time to only what is necessary should accompany its use. Jesus advocates for a very radical approach to dealing with the cause of the sin of lust. In His perspective, it would be better for a person to suffer the loss of something useful to them than to continue on in sin and have their entire body cast into hell because of a lack of willingness to deal severely with the "cause" of the sin.

*"For our fight is not against any physical enemy:
it is against organizations and powers that are spiritual.
We are up against the unseen power that controls this dark
world, and spiritual agents from the very headquarters
of evil."* (Ephesians 6:12 PHP)

The woman who is determined to overcome habitual sexual sin must prepare herself to battle through and combat her old nature which still longs for the pleasure of sexual sin. Not only does her flesh desire it, but a habit of indulgence has been well established. Throughout a Christian woman's daily life, she discovers that our culture promotes a resounding message that unlawful sex is a good and desirable thing that provides endless possibilities to satisfy every fantasy imaginable. As if all of this were not enough, the struggling woman must realize and accept the fact that there is a highly organized army of powerful beings who are dedicated to thwart her attainment of freedom.

It is very important for the woman who struggles to have a proper understanding of her real enemies in this spiritual battle. There are those who believe that the entire difficulty in overcoming habitual sin is only a result of spiritual warfare, thereby minimizing the role of the flesh and the world. We once had a conversation with a minister about sexual lust. After briefly telling him of our work with sexual addicts, he replied,

172 CREATE IN ME A PURE HEART

"When I deal with someone in sexual sin I just cast the demon out and I'm done with it!"

Steve responded, "Yes, I understand that demons can affect people in some ways, but until a person learns to deal with his own flesh, casting a legion of devils out of him will not solve his problem."

Many who operate in the area of deliverance greatly over-emphasize the role demons play in habitual sin. They seem to be looking for an easy answer, or perhaps they are simply enthralled with the idea of ordering demons around.

At the opposite end of the spectrum are those who claim that all of a struggling woman's problems can be attributed only to herself. This is equally wrong. The idea of there being demonic forces at work in this world is a concept that they prefer not to think about. Their perspective of the spiritual realm tends to be extremely vague and shallow. They would never refute what the Bible says about the enemy, but they are inclined to limit demonic activity to witch doctors in some dark village in Africa.

The truth is that there is a sophisticated army of beings who operate under the auspices of the devil himself. Most scholars believe that Satan was one of the twelve original archangels created by God. He is not simply an "evil force" or an "evil influence" as some believe. He is an angelic being who, like humans, is limited to time and space. However, unlike man, he is a spiritual being who is not confined to the limits of physical matter.

His army is composed of demons of various sizes, strengths, abilities, and functions. (See Luke 11:14; Matthew 12:22; I John 4:6) They range from princes of countries, (Daniel 10:13) down to lowly soldiers. (Luke 8:30) Paul gives an indication of this intricate hierarchy in the Book of Ephesians, "For our struggle is not against flesh and blood, but against the rulers, against the powers, against the world forces of this darkness, against the spiritual forces of wickedness in the heavenly places." (Ephesians 6:12)

Like any military outfit, it seems as though there are generals,

CHAPTER TWELVE:
BATTLES IN THE SPIRITUAL REALM

captains, and soldiers—or at least some equivalent thereof—and that demons have been specially assigned to harass and attack individuals. This is mostly conjecture of course, but apparently the designated demon will be selected on the basis of that person's particular area of struggle. To the one who struggles with depression, a devil of dark gloom would be appointed. For those who battle a hot temper, a spirit of rage or murder would be given the task; and for an exaggerated sex drive, an unclean spirit would be commissioned. It is likely that these demons have the ability to create spiritual atmospheres which are conducive to an individual's struggle. The renowned Dr. Merrill F. Unger, a professor of Old Testament Studies at Dallas Theological Seminary for twenty years, says the following about demonic activity in his book *Demons in the World Today*:

> In demon influence, evil spirits exert power over a person short of actual possession. Such influence may vary from mild harassment to extreme subjection when body and mind become dominated and held in slavery by spirit agents. Christians, as well as non-Christians, can be so influenced. They may be oppressed, vexed, depressed, hindered, and bound by demons.[1]

Under God's Umbrella

Regardless of their specialty, demons are limited in their sphere of influence and license to harass or torment a believer. As a child of God, one should always be mindful of the fact that Satan and his cohorts can do no more than what is allowed by the Lord and His spiritual laws.

There are certain laws which govern the physical realm dictating how humans must conduct the activities of their daily lives. Light a match under a dry sheet of paper, and it will burn because certain components have been introduced together which result in fire. Drop a bowling ball out of a window, and it will fall until something stops its progress. These are examples of cause-and-effect laws, and there are many which we must deal with in the physical realm everyday. Much of what we do in life is dictated by various physical rules of nature.

By the same token, there are spiritual laws which govern the invisible realm around us. Paul described one of these in the Book of Galatians. "Do not be deceived, God is not mocked; for whatever a man sows, this he will also reap. For the one who sows to his own flesh shall from the flesh reap corruption, but the one who sows to the Spirit shall from the Spirit reap eternal life." (Galatians 6:7-8) This spiritual law states that when a person commits an act, he must endure the consequences which will follow. Jesus gives another example of a rule of the kingdom of God, "And whoever exalts himself shall be humbled; and whoever humbles himself shall be exalted." (Matthew 23:12) It does not matter if someone approves or disapproves of these laws, nor does it matter if they are highly regarded. These are cause-and-effect rules of the kingdom of God that cannot be escaped.

There also seems to be spiritual laws regarding the involvement of demonic forces in the lives of believers. When a Christian rebels against God's kingdom by committing a willful act of sin, he is aligning himself with the enemy. The Apostle John said, "the one who practices sin is of the devil." (I John 3:8) The primary point of this statement is, simply, that the person who *habitually* transgresses God's laws is in league with Satan—the great rebel himself. However, there is a secondary truth which can be drawn from this statement. As a person commits acts of sin he is opening himself up to a greater degree of influence by the enemy. For instance, if a Christian woman enters a pornographic website, she has willfully made herself vulnerable to the devilish thoughts that will plague her for weeks to come. Once the woman has "opened herself up" to pornography, devils have the "legal right" to continually attack and torment her with those pornographic images.

Another example is anger. When a person's will is crossed, there is a huge temptation to rise up in anger. Anger is an emotion of the flesh which generally emerges out of pride. Some have "bad tempers," meaning they habitually allow themselves to be dominated by anger. It is wrong for a follower of the lowly Jesus to get mad at someone, but when that person lets that anger control him or her to the point of rage, they have given place to a devil. Paul said, "Be angry, and yet do not sin; do not let the sun go down on your anger, and do not give the devil an opportunity" (Ephesians 4:26-27), or as it is expressed in the NIV, "…do not give the devil a foothold." Anger, like lust, is a carnal impulse which the enemy seeks to intensify in a person's life. Dr. Unger states:

> Demon influence may occur in different degrees of severity and in a variety of forms, both in Christians and non-Christians. In its less severe forms, demon attack comes from without through pressure, suggestion, and temptation. When such pressure, suggestion, and temptation are yielded to, the result is always an increased degree of demon influence. Although the human race fell in Adam and became a prey to Satan and demons, the forces of darkness have always been severely restricted. They can enslave and oppress fallen man only to the degree he willingly violates the eternal moral law of God and exposes himself to evil.[2]

Those who foolishly open the door to sexual sin can expect the enemy to take full advantage of the opportunity to bring the person into a greater place of bondage. Merlin Carothers, well known for his popular teachings on praise, tells of demonic influence on the thought life:

But any thought connected with illicit sex is like a monster waiting to take over. It can be kept hidden for many years, but at the right moment it emerges. In fact this evil force is often willing to wait for the right moment to manifest itself. It wants to damage the greatest number of people possible. Does this frighten you?

Let me assure you that I'm not talking about evil spirits possessing Christians. There exists in this world an evil force whose desire is to destroy everything God wants to build, however. That force, Satan, is far more clever than the average Christian believes. Satan leads his people to live in open rebellion against God, but he is content to work secretly in the inward parts of Christians. His strategy is to entice us to want things that God has forbidden. Once the desire is created, Satan keeps fortifying that desire. He repeatedly brings it to our attention until it outweighs our desire to be obedient to God…

It is never safe to step into Satan's territory. He goes about seeking whom he may devour. He selects his own time to accomplish his own purposes. We never know what he will do. I've had men tell me that they lived with immoral thoughts and desires for twenty-five years before they yielded to immoral acts. Time is irrelevant to Satan. If you believe that he is a reality, and that he has spiritual power, it will profit you greatly to stay out of his territory! He, too, has a plan for you and it very likely will be fulfilled if you allow any part of your life to be under his control. He is especially interested in what's on your mind.[3]

The attacks of devils are not limited to the guilty, though. The innocent are sometimes assaulted. However, no attack can occur upon a believer without the consent of God. Take, for instance, the time Jesus told Peter, "Simon, Simon, behold, Satan has demanded permission to sift you like wheat; but I have prayed for you, that your faith may not fail." (Luke 22:31-32) Once the person belongs to God, the enemy can demand all he wants, but he must have permission before he can attack. Believers have been purchased from the devil by the blood of Jesus.

A profound picture of this is shown to us in the first chapter of the Book of Job. In this section of Scripture the reader is given a fascinating glimpse into the unseen regions of the spiritual realm where great temptations are devised. Job is described as a man who "was blameless, upright, fearing God, and turning away from evil." It goes on to say that he lived in such a state of righteousness that whenever his sons would get together for a feast, he would offer up a special sacrifice to God, thinking "perhaps my sons have sinned and cursed God in their hearts."

After establishing the godly character of Job, the scene shifts to the throne room of the Almighty where Satan slithers in amongst the other angels. Beaming with a certain parental pride, God says, "Have you considered My servant Job? For there is no one like him on the earth, a blameless and upright man, fearing God and turning away from evil."

To this the devil rasps, "Does Job fear God for nothing? Hast Thou not made a hedge about him and his house and all that he has, on every side? Thou hast blessed the work of his hands, and his possessions have increased in the land. But put forth Thy hand now and touch all that he has; he will surely curse Thee to Thy face." So, unbeknownst to this upright man on earth, a dare uttered in an entirely different realm is about to result in Job's whole life being turned upside-down.

One of the reasons this story was put into Scripture was to show believers that our Heavenly Father has established boundaries that the enemy cannot cross without His permission.*

---

* For a study into God's sovereign designs in allowing trials and temptations, see the author's book *Living in Victory*.

Masters at Temptation

Demonic beings have been tempting, harassing and attacking believers since the inception of mankind. They use unsaved humans to act out the deeds of hatred, arrogance, and perversion which are all part of their evil natures. This is the eternity that the unsaved can expect.

Those who are on the pathway of following God are dealt with somewhat differently. As mentioned before, demons are restricted in their level of influence. The Marines who were involved in espionage in Moscow in the 1980's will serve as a good illustration. The only thing these embassy guards had to be concerned about was allowing themselves to be duped into telling secrets. Russian agents were confined to operate within certain boundaries. They could not use torture to force the Marines to pass along military information. They could not threaten their lives or even yell at them. The only possible way they could obtain secrets was through the process of seduction. That is precisely what they did. The Russians used a beautiful woman as their ploy to entice a Marine into revealing secrets. This Marine did not place his country above himself. He may have been willing to die for his country on a battlefield, but he was unwilling to die to his own desires. He lost the biggest battle he would ever face. It was not a battle involving bullets; it was a battle with temptation.

In the same way, when the enemy determines to plot the downfall of a believer, he can only work within the boundaries set forth by God. As Paul pointed out, "No temptation has overtaken you but such as is common to man; and God is faithful, who will not allow you to be tempted beyond what you are able, but with the temptation will provide the way of escape also, that you may be able to endure it." (I Corinthians 10:13) The veteran Apostle does not promise a life free of temptations, but rather that God will keep them within His limits and always provide a way of escape in order that the believer may continue to stand.

The scene we witnessed in the book of Job is typical of what occurs when a fallen spirit desires to sift one of God's children. Take, for instance, the story of Joseph and Potiphar's wife. We are only given the earthly picture of what occurred, but what happened in the spiritual realm preceding this incident? I can easily imagine the serpent once again slithering into the throne room of God. "Does Joseph fear God for nothing? Hast Thou not made a hedge about him and his house and all that he has, on every side? Thou hast blessed the work of his hands, and his possessions have increased in the land. But allow me to tempt him with this beautiful woman, and he will turn his back on You. But if for some reason he doesn't, allow me to have him thrown into prison, and he will surely curse Thee to Thy face." I suspect a similar conversation did in fact occur prior to the great temptation Joseph faced that day. Consequently, the temptation an individual faces, regardless of what it may be, must *first* be permitted by the Lord.

Pulling Down Strongholds

When a woman gives in to sexual sin repeatedly over a period of time, a foothold is established by the enemy within that woman's being. If that sin continues to a point that it is uncontrollable, it becomes a stronghold of the enemy. A devil of perversion has set up a fortress within the soulish realm of the woman. The longer the sin continues, the more fortified the presence becomes. **

** Although many like to take positions for or against the possibility of a Christian being demon-possessed, it seems best to understand the Scriptures as simply referring to individuals who are *demonized* (rather than possessed). Certainly, even a Christian can be demonized to some degree, and more importantly, it seems apparent that habitual sin strengthens the ability of demons to tempt the addict into that particular sin.

We have made a few visits to the Golan Heights at various times over the years. One can easily understand why Israel has been reluctant to surrender this small area to the Syrians. Enemy forces had taken their time to become firmly entrenched in the side of the hills overlooking the Sea of Galilee. For many years they had bombarded the Israeli settlements below. When war broke out in 1967 between Israel and the Arab nations surrounding her, it took fierce fighting to dislodge the Syrian presence above the lake. Buried under tons of concrete, their artillery must have seemed invincible to the Jews.

This is what the saint feels like who must face the intimidating prospect of dislodging an enemy buried deep within his or her being. Although this may seem quite overwhelming, Paul assures us that it is not the case: "For though we walk in the flesh, we do not war after the flesh: (For the weapons of our warfare are not carnal, but mighty through God to the pulling down of strong holds;) Casting down imaginations, and every high thing that exalteth itself against the knowledge of God, and bringing into captivity every thought to the obedience of Christ." (II Corinthians 10:3-5 KJV)

Much of the remainder of this book will teach principles required to oust the enemy. There is no real need to discuss it at length now. We simply mention it here so that you can better understand the battle which lies ahead. However, it would be good to note what Paul said about the place which fantasy plays in establishing and maintaining a stronghold. The enemy will maintain his position only to the extent that the woman continues to entertain sexual or romantic fantasies. Paul tells us to cast those imaginations down. It may take time before the woman has a pure thought life, but it is vital that she begins to exercise mental discipline now. Peter said, "Therefore, gird your minds for action, keep sober in spirit, fix your hope completely on the grace to be brought to you at the revelation of Jesus Christ. As obedient children, do not be conformed to the former lusts which were yours in your ignorance, but like the Holy One who called you, be holy yourselves also in all your behavior; because it is written, 'you shall be holy, for I am holy.'" (I Peter 1:13-16)

The Schemes of the Devil

Victory is a vague concept to those who have become accustomed to losing spiritual battles. They have mostly known only defeat. There seems to be no power to resist seducing spirits with their seemingly irresistible temptations. However, the power is available for the child of God to withstand the adversary. Paul ministered a long time in the city of Ephesus, where much of the church congregation consisted of former devil-worshipers. These were people who had to face the enemy in an extremely wicked environment. From his prison cell in Rome, the old warrior wrote the epistle which has come to be known as Ephesians. In it he gave the following treatise on spiritual warfare:

Finally, be strong in the Lord, and in the strength of His might. Put on the full armor of God, that you may be able to stand firm against the schemes of the devil. For our struggle is not against flesh and blood, but against the rulers, against the powers, against the world forces of this darkness, against the spiritual forces of wickedness in the heavenly places. Therefore, take up the full armor of God, that you may be able to resist in the evil day, and having done everything, to stand firm. Stand firm therefore, having girded your loins with truth, and having put on the breastplate of righteousness, and having shod your feet with the preparation of the gospel of peace; in addition to all, taking up the shield of faith with which you will be able to extinguish all the flaming missiles of the evil one. And take the helmet of salvation, and the sword of the Spirit, which is the word of God. With all prayer and petition pray at all times in the Spirit, and with this in view, be on the alert with all perseverance and petition for all the saints. (Ephesians 6:10-18)

The first thing Paul established was the source of all believers' power to fight the enemy. The Amplified Bible brings out the full meaning of what he was expressing in verse ten: "...be empowered through your union with Him; draw your strength from Him—that strength which His [boundless] might provides." Paul was touching here on a subject of enormous importance: spiritual battles are not fought with one's own strength or abilities. I know it sounds ridiculous to express it in such a simple way, but we need to be reminded that spiritual warfare is indeed spiritual! As Paul said in the passage in II Corinthians, "For though we walk in the flesh, we do not war after the flesh." The degree to which the battle is fought in the spirit realm is the degree to which warfare will be effective. For believers, the source of their spiritual power is the Holy Spirit.

This leads us to another important truth regarding the power of God. He will only demonstrate His power in our lives to the extent that we are weak in ourselves. Our weakness creates a true dependence upon God. In the last three chapters of Paul's second epistle to the church at Corinth, he used the word weakness thirteen times—in several instances to describe himself. He was trying to teach the Corinthians that spiritual power is different from personal power. His critics had said that "his personal presence is unimpressive, and his speech contemptible." (II Corinthians 10:10) Paul did not deny this, but simply responded by quoting Jeremiah, "He who boasts, let him boast in the Lord."

In the eleventh chapter of II Corinthians, Paul recorded all the suffering he had undergone through preaching the gospel: beatings, whippings, stonings, shipwrecks, constant dangers, hunger, and thirst. God permitted these afflictions in order to keep Paul weak and dependent upon Him. In the twelfth chapter, Paul tells how God had to further weaken him through "a thorn in the flesh" so that he could continue to pour out His power through Paul's life. God said to him, "My grace is sufficient for you, for power is perfected in weakness." To this Paul responded, "Most gladly, therefore, I will rather boast about my weaknesses, that the power of Christ may dwell in me." (II Corinthians 12:9) *The only way a believer will defeat the enemy in the area of spiritual temptation is through the power of God.* That power is appropriated through the believer's utter dependence upon Him.

Thus, we see in Ephesians six that our power comes through our close fellowship with the Lord. Paul goes on to say, "Put on the full armor of God..." Why should we put on this armor? "...that you may be able to stand firm against the schemes of the devil." The principles Paul is about to share with the Ephesians is for the purpose of helping them to avoid the crafty plans the devil devises to lead believers astray. When examining the various articles of armor, one can quickly see that most are defensive in nature: girdle, breastplate, shield, and helmet are all for the purpose of protecting oneself from the blows of the opponent. It could even be argued that the sword is defensive, in the sense that a person uses it to deflect the opponent's weapons.***

Again, the purpose for putting on the armor is so "that you may be able to stand firm against the schemes of the devil." In the thirteenth verse, Paul reemphasizes this by saying, "Therefore, take up the full armor of God, that you may be able to resist in the evil day..." The exhortation is intentionally repeated to exhort us to stand against the temptations presented by demons, whatever the cost may be.

*** A perfect picture of this is given us by the Lord Himself when He countered the devil's temptations by quoting the Word of God (Matthew 4: 4, 7, 10).

Sleeping With the Enemy

While speaking with the disciples one day, Jesus said, "I will not speak much more with you, for the ruler of the world is coming, and he has nothing in Me." (John 14:30) Jesus revealed within this one statement the reason He was able to "stand firm against the schemes of the devil." He said the ruler of this world had *nothing* in Him. In other words, there was nothing in His life that was outside of the Father's will. There was no sin, rebellion, or secret habits. Satan did not have a "hook" in Jesus. There was absolutely nothing in Jesus which the devil had legal grounds to use against Him.

This is the place of refuge for the believer. If a woman stays in God's will and remains obedient to Him, the enemy is unable to lure her into rebellion. Believers experience problems when they give in to foul spirits in small ways, making small alliances with those who are their enemies. If they have areas of common ground with the enemy, how will they stand? It is every Christian woman's responsibility to keep herself untainted by the pollutions of this world system through the grace of God. (James 1:27) The sinful nature may want to befriend unclean spirits, but by habitual acts of the will, the woman can choose to remain in fellowship with God by being obedient to Him; and as she does, the devil has nothing in her.

The armor of God is, in one sense, a protection to the woman from *herself*. As she establishes the principles of truth, righteousness, faith, and so on, she will grow spiritually and will be empowered to resist the temptations which appeal to her sinful nature. The real victory in the woman's life depends, not necessarily on how she responds to today's temptations, but on how willing she is to allow God to change her from the inside out. Although this growth does not come overnight, the process often must begin through one isolated experience.

CREATE IN ME A PURE HEART
Part 4: THE WAY OUT

CHAPTER THIRTEEN:
THE PLACE OF BROKENNESS AND REPENTANCE

"At the name of Jesus every knee should bow...
and every tongue confess that Jesus Christ is Lord."
(Philippians 2:10-11 NLT)

I (Steve) was invited to do an interview on one of the premier Christian radio talk shows about sexual addiction in the Church. During the days preceding the interview, I felt a growing conviction to convey to the radio audience the message that God changes people. I was determined to make the point that a person bound up in sexual sin has hope because of the transforming power of Jesus Christ.

However, the host of the program was equally determined to communicate his philosophy. His belief was that freedom from addiction rested upon the foundation of mutual accountability amongst others who are addicted. Each time I attempted to move the conversation to the transforming power of God, which can truly set all addicts free from their bondage, he would divert my efforts and emphasize the need for accountability. While accountability has its place in the restoration process, it is certainly not the most important aspect to overcoming an addiction.

The answer for the woman struggling with sexual sin is that God changes people from the inside out. This change occurs as the woman sees her need for change, comes to grip with her sinful behavior, and experiences a genuine turning away from that lifestyle. Such a transformation does not merely involve quitting sin. It is much deeper than just abstinence. In order for God to get a woman to the place where she is able to forsake the idols of her life, a tremendous upheaval of her entire inner life is necessary. She has cherished and protected her idol over the years because she loves and desires it. God's task is to gradually bring her to the place where she no longer desires it. Those who attempt to keep their sin in abeyance while maintaining control of the rest of their lives will never find real freedom.

A revolution must take place before a woman will hate her sin. A new King must be inaugurated. The old kingdom, under the reign of self, must be toppled. The woman who becomes a follower of Christ and attempts to maintain control over her own life has not submitted herself to the lordship of Jesus Christ. All this woman can ever hope for is to abstain from her besetting sin. On the other hand, the woman who has allowed God to break down self rule, has a whole new set of values infused into her being. This is what Paul was referring to when he said, "Therefore if any man be in Christ, he is a new creature: old things are passed away; behold, all things are become new." (II Corinthians 5:17) He gave a fuller version of what he was expressing in his letter to the Ephesian church:

> This I say therefore, and affirm together with the Lord, that you walk no longer just as the Gentiles also walk, in the futility of their mind, being darkened in their understanding, excluded from the life of God, because of the ignorance that is in them, because of the hardness of their heart; and they, having become callous, have given themselves over to sensuality, for the practice of every kind of impurity with greediness.
>
> But you did not learn Christ in this way, if indeed

you have heard Him and have been taught in Him, just as truth is in Jesus, that, in reference to your former manner of life, you lay aside the old self, which is being corrupted in accordance with the lusts of deceit, and that you be renewed in the spirit of your mind, and put on the new self, which in the likeness of God has been created in righteousness and holiness of the truth. (Ephesians 4:17-24)

Dealing with Self-Will

Every human being possesses an innate sense of self-determination and self-sufficiency. When a woman becomes a follower of Christ, she has set herself on an unavoidable collision course with the will of God, regardless of the severity of her sin. Indeed, the very entrance into the kingdom of God is predicated upon the woman seeing that her way has been wrong and must therefore be changed. The biblical term used to describe the solution to this problem is called REPENTANCE.

It is a subject of enormous importance in the New Testament. Jesus preached that an entrance into the Kingdom of God required both repentance and faith. (Mark 1:15) Repentance was the first thing He preached (Matthew 4:17) and the last thing He commanded. (Revelation 3:19) In fact, in this second reference, He urged people to exercise zeal in their repentance. We might ask ourselves how zealous we are about seeing the need to continually turn away from sin and the ways of self and turn toward the Lord. There is a great need for ongoing repentance in the life of the believer because she still has a flesh nature which must be broken of its power and conquered by the Holy Spirit.

True repentance then, is much more than aligning oneself with the Christian religion. The Greek word which we translate as repentance is *metanoia*. It is the combination of the words *meta* (after, following) and *noieo* (think). *Metanoia* means to reconsider, or to experience a change in one's line of thinking and, subsequently, one's behavior.

Before we discuss repentance of sexual sin, let us return to the matter of the human will. It is sheer nonsense for a woman to believe that she can repent of some particular sin without changing her way of thinking. *Spiritual repentance is an experience whereby a person's will is altered for the express purpose of bringing it into line with God's will.*

Let me use a couple of stories out of the life of Jesus to illustrate the difference between real repentance and false repentance. One day Jesus noticed a young man intently listening to Him. He made that wondrous invitation for the young guy to follow Him. "I will follow You, Lord; but first permit me to say good-bye to those at home." Jesus replied to him, "No one, after putting his hand to the plow and looking back, is fit for the kingdom of God." (Luke 9:61-62) The man expressed his will: "I will; it is my express desire to follow You…but it is also my desire to spend time with loved ones first. I wish to be your follower, but it must be on my own terms."

How different is the story of Zaccheus who was so dramatically affected by his encounter with the Messiah he exclaimed, "Behold, Lord, half of my possessions *I will* give to the poor, and if I have defrauded anyone of anything, *I will* give back four times as much." His will had been changed to conform to the will of God. This is the repentance the other one did not experience. When Jesus saw his response He proclaimed, "Today salvation has come to this house." (Luke 19:9)

Jesus later told a story to illustrate the difference between true and false repentance.

"But what do you think? A man had two sons, and he came to the first and said, 'Son, go work today in the vineyard.' And he answered and said, 'I will, sir,' and he did not go. And he came to the second and said the

same thing. But he answered and said, 'I will not,' yet
he afterward regretted it and went. Which of the two
did the will of his father?" They said, "The latter." Jesus
said to them, "Truly I say to you that the tax-gatherers
and harlots will get into the kingdom of God before
you." (Matthew 21:28-31)

In this passage of Scripture, the first son conveyed the
impression that he would do the will of his father: "I will, sir,"
he stated. Though he represented himself as one who intended
to do the will of his father, he failed to follow through. Perhaps
he was the double-minded man who is unstable in all of his ways
that James would later talk about; or perhaps he was someone
who lived a façade of outward obedience without it being the
reality of his life. Whatever the case may be, he did not obey
his father.

The second son, on the other hand, refused from the outset.
"It is my will not to do as you wish," he said. Later, having
thought better of his decision, he changed his mind. Jesus said
that he *regretted* his thinking. Perhaps the moral of the story could
best be summed up in the words of Jesus during the Sermon
on the Mount: "Not everyone who says to Me, 'Lord, Lord,'
will enter the kingdom of heaven; but he who does the will of
My Father who is in heaven." (Matthew 7:21) In other words, a
mere verbal claiming of obedience does not equate to the actual
performance of it.

The woman who wishes to live a life of obedience but
continually fails must deal with her will. She sees herself as
under the power of some foreign entity (whether she considers
it demonic or simply sin), but in reality she is under the power of
her own will. She is much like the spoiled child who is continually
naughty. There are times when she wants to be a good girl, but
when something comes along that she wants to do, she does

it regardless of the consequences. She is undisciplined. She is accustomed to having her own way. She, rather than her Father, is the master of her life. The woman in habitual sexual sin conducts herself in much the same manner. She does whatever she wishes to do. She desires to commit acts of sexual sin because she enjoys it.

As we will discover in the remaining chapters, there are a number of aspects involved in a woman coming into a life of freedom. One of the key elements of the process involves repentance: *having one's will altered to bring it into subjection and consecration to the will of God.* As Paul said, "For this is the will of God, your sanctification; that is, that you abstain from sexual immorality; that each of you know how to possess his own vessel in sanctification and honor, not in lustful passion, like the Gentiles who do not know God...For God has not called us for the purpose of impurity, but in sanctification. So, he who rejects *this* is not rejecting man but the God who gives His Holy Spirit to you." (I Thessalonians 4:3-8)

Repentance describes the transforming of a woman from being one who does her own (carnal) will, to one who does the will of her Father. At the beginning of His ministry, the first words out of the mouth of Jesus were, "Repent, for the kingdom of heaven is at hand." (Matthew 4:17) He then went on to give the fabulous Sermon on the Mount, which is a description of the initial experience of repentance and the lifestyle that emerges as a result. The Beatitudes contain all that is involved in the process of transformation. Those seven verses, Matthew 5:3-9, describe how a person is prepared for repentance, how it unfolds, and the life that accompanies it.

Seeing One's Need for Change

Jesus opens His revolutionary sermon with the words, "Blessed are the poor in spirit, for theirs is the kingdom of heaven." (Matthew 5:3) These words describe the condition of an individual's heart who becomes aware of her great need for God's work in her life. The one who has a real conversion to Christ experiences the overwhelming sense of being utterly undone. A woman, at least at this point in her life, comes to see that there is nothing she can possibly do to save herself. She realizes that only the blood of Jesus Christ can provide the atonement for her sin.

The woman who is overwhelmed with a sense of complete powerlessness over her sin often has a sense of what it means to be poor in spirit. She has tried to quit her sinful behavior many times, making countless resolutions. She has tried with all her strength to change her life. When temptations would come along, like a little child being led by the hand, she would blindly follow the dictates of her lust. This woman can see that her only hope for deliverance from the power of sin is the Savior.

Many understand, in a vague way, that they cannot overcome their sin but never experience true poverty of spirit. To be poor in spirit means that one truly sees no ability within oneself to overcome the power of sin apart from God's help. Those who try to "maintain" their sin have never come into a true sight of their helplessness. They will not acknowledge their need because they wish to remain in control of their own lives. When a woman has truly seen her helpless condition, she is desperate for God's help no matter what it may cost her.

While there are many who never come to this place of poverty, others arrive and never go any further. They live their lives openly confessing their helplessness but unbelief stymies their spiritual progress. It is not enough that a woman realizes she cannot overcome the sin on her own; something must take place inside her.

The Breaking of Self-Will

Once a woman sees her sinful condition there is but one reasonable response: deep sorrow over how much she has disobeyed, offended, defied, and yes, even hurt the Lord. The second phrase Jesus uttered in His Sermon on the Mount was, "Blessed are those who mourn, for they shall be comforted." (Matthew 5:4)

When a woman begins to experience true godly sorrow over her sin, a change begins to occur in her heart. She literally begins to hate her sin, realizing its evil, deceitful nature which has kept her out of real fellowship with God and other believers. Paul said of the Corinthians who finally repented, "I now rejoice, not that you were made sorrowful, but that you were made sorrowful to the point of repentance; for you were made sorrowful according to the will of God…For the sorrow that is according to the will of God produces a repentance without regret, leading to salvation; but the sorrow of the world produces death." (II Corinthians 7:9-10)

Throughout the years we have counseled many who had only worldly sorrow. Jesus spoke of peace that the world gives. (John 14:27) There is also a sorrow that the world gives and the two are closely connected. Worldly peace depends upon favorable outward circumstances. The peace Jesus gives is a sense of inner tranquility that only comes through being in an undisturbed relationship with God.

Worldly sorrow is the grief due to unfavorable circumstances. Sexual sin can quickly bring such circumstances about. Financial debts often pile up; a devastated husband may file for divorce; or a secret life might be exposed on the job or even in the church. Feeling tremendous remorse over one's actions because of the consequences that have followed is not uncommon. We truly empathize with those who must face the consequences of their sexual misconduct. Nonetheless, such regret is common to any of the human race who encounter unfavorable circumstances. That is what is called by Paul, "worldly sorrow." It is not wrong to feel grief over these losses. It is only natural to feel badly when in an ill-suited predicament. The danger with worldly sorrow, however, is that it gives one a false sense of brokenness and repentance. Consequently, Paul says it leads to death.

How different is the woman who experiences true godly sorrow! Yes, though she grieves the consequences of her sin, there is something different taking place inside of her. A deeper, more genuine remorse penetrates her heart which has been hardened for so long. She sees what her sin has done to her family. She becomes overwhelmed by the enormity of her selfish lifestyle. Her pride stares at her glaringly. She is reminded of how unconcerned she has been about others. She realizes that she has grieved a loving God. She has repeatedly wounded other people. The pleasure of her sin has come at a tremendous price. Everywhere she turns she sees the devastation of her sin. This is not the selfish whining of a person in worldly sorrow. This woman is being broken over *who she is*. The control she has had over her life has destroyed most everything of value to her. This is a woman who can see all too clearly the price of self-will. True repentance is a profound and powerful experience (or ongoing phenomena). How shallow in comparison those empty resolutions that many have made under the term repentance!

I (Steve) have had numerous breakings in my life. Perhaps the one that affected me the most happened in 1991. I had been in ministry for five years at that time. Even though I had long since overcome habitual sexual sin and had even been used by the Lord to some extent, I was still very selfish and prideful. I was spending a couple of hours in prayer and Bible study every morning, but I could feel myself getting distant from the Lord. When I prayed it seemed as though God was a million miles away. The heavens had become brass to me. The Bible seemed dry and stale. I was growing increasingly cynical of others, hardened to the Lord, and cold to the needs of those to whom I was called to minister.

Pure Life Ministries had recently purchased a larger piece of property (where we are currently located) and needed to find a new church for the men in the live-in program to attend. One Sunday, Kathy and I attended a small Pentecostal church out in the country, not far from the new facility. I was there to decide if it was the kind of church we would want the men to attend.

The pastor preached that day out of Luke chapter six. It was not so much what he was saying that moved me as it was that God was showing me that I was not living the Christian life. No, I was not stirred emotionally, but I felt convicted. At the end of the sermon he gave an altar call for anybody who felt that they needed to get right with God. In my prideful condition, the last thing I wanted to do was to respond to an altar call. I was there to check the church out, not to repent! In spite of my reluctance, I knew that I had to obey the Lord's voice.

As soon as my knees hit the floor at the altar, I began to weep. All I could see was how very prideful and arrogant I had been. I saw the lack of mercy and love in my life. The more God showed me, the more I wept. Pretty soon deep sobs were wracking my whole frame. In front of this entire congregation, which I had been so concerned about impressing, I was blubbering like a baby! The more I cried, the more humiliated I felt. The more humiliated I felt, the more I cried.

It was a terrible experience in the flesh and yet was one of the greatest days in my life! My prideful thinking, selfish nature, and stubborn will were all dealt a severe, but precise, blow. Out of that experience came a new brokenness that completely transformed my thinking. It was not that I would never give in to pride or selfishness again; they just lost their uncontested power over my life.

This kind of brokenness is what the woman in sexual sin desperately needs to experience. The strong will (like the spoiled child who always gets his way) must be dealt with severely by the Lord. God must be given His rightful position of authority in the woman's heart. This dethronement of the "almighty self" can only take place through such brokenness.

Each time one is broken by God, self loses that much control over one's life. The old nature, which loves the pleasures of sin, must be crushed. This can only come about through the mighty hand of God. We will discuss this in more detail later but mention it now as an important part in the process of repentance.

The woman who attempts to "maintain" her sin cannot have true victory because her *heart* has not changed! Those who tell you that you must spend the rest of your life in support groups and in therapy do not understand God's power to transform a repentant heart. Many of them will never know about repentance because they will not allow *themselves* to be broken by God. Thus, their own hardened, unbroken hearts establish the basis for what they teach others. Out of that stony ground comes the kind of teachings that promote weak repentance.

The Conquered Will

The third Beatitude spoken by Jesus is, "Blessed are the meek, for they will inherit the earth." (Matthew 5:5 NIV) Meekness is the willing subjection of one person's will to the will of another. Jesus lived in absolute meekness. He was perfectly submitted to the Father. "For I have come down from heaven, not to do My own will, but the will of Him who sent Me," He told His followers. (John 6:38). In fact, on another occasion He said, "I can do nothing on My own initiative. As I hear, I judge; and My judgment is just, because I do not seek My own will, but the will of Him who sent Me." (John 5:30)

Jesus did not need to be broken because He did not have a fallen human nature. He was born with His Father's sinless nature. It is a different matter for the sons and daughters of Adam. The only way we can come into meekness is through the breaking of our wills. A perfect picture of this is that of a stallion. It may be a beautiful and graceful animal, but it has no usefulness until it has been broken. However, once it has been broken, the powerful horse becomes controlled by the reins and verbal commands of its master. This is a picture of biblical meekness.

The Christian woman who has undergone the crushing of her will by her Heavenly Father has learned to have a healthy respect for the Master's whip. This is not the cowering fear an abused child has of a cruel father, but the proper reverence one has to One who commands respect. This woman's will has been conquered so that she no longer sees her life as one in which she has the right to control. "Or do you not know that your body is a temple of the Holy Spirit who is in you, whom you have from God, and that you are not your own? For you have been bought with a price: therefore glorify God in your body." (I Corinthians 6:19-20)

The fear of God establishes certain perimeters around the woman, which helps to hinder any venturing into the unlawful territory of sexual sin. Righteousness is the result. "Blessed are those who hunger and thirst for righteousness, for they shall be satisfied," Jesus went on to say. (Matthew 5:6) The woman who learns to live her life under the ever-present gaze of a holy God, longs to please Him. The Lord describes that longing as hungering and thirsting after righteousness. Such a desire to please God promotes a genuine hatred for sin and a willingness to overthrow all of one's idols.

Jesus proceeds to describe mercy, purity and peacemaking, which further characterize the life of a person who has experienced real brokenness and repentance. As the person's hardened, unmerciful heart is crushed, a new compassion and love for others replaces it. It is the new life which Paul described. However, this initial breaking by God is just the beginning!

CHAPTER FOURTEEN:
DISCIPLINED FOR HOLINESS

*"Let us make ourselves clean from all evil of flesh
and spirit, and become completely holy in the
fear of God." (II Corinthians 7:1 BBE)*

When you get right down to it, anyone in habitual sin lacks self-discipline in at least one area of their lives. Discipline is greatly needed in a woman's life, though the thought of it might make her cringe.

Discipline has been defined as, "Learning that molds character and enforces correct behavior…To discipline a person or a group means to put them in a state of good order so that they function in the way intended."[1] The Bible uses the term fool to describe a man who does not heed instruction nor receive "the life-giving reproof." Though discipline is the very thing which can help him out of the chaos he has created in his life, he refuses to receive it. Solomon said, "…Fools despise wisdom and instruction," (Proverbs 1:7) "hate knowledge" (Proverbs 1:22) and are "arrogant and careless." (Proverbs 14:16) "Do not speak in the hearing of a fool," Solomon instructed, "for he will despise the wisdom of your words." (Proverbs 23:9) He also said, "A fool does not delight in understanding, but only in revealing his own mind." (Proverbs 18:2) Part of the reason a sexual addict is uninterested in receiving correction is because his mind "is in the house of pleasure." (Ecclesiastes 7:4)

Christians whose lives have been ravaged by sin will humbly admit that these verses accurately describe the way they have been in the past. Many sought help, but were always looking for a painless, easy answer. They were drawn to "solutions" that required little and yet promised much. Or they were drawn to "touchy, feel-good" books that made them feel as though they were victims rather than sinners. Of course, in today's society, there is never a shortage of self-proclaimed experts who boldly offer an easy way out of whatever issue or circumstance individuals commonly face in life.

Truthfully, there is no easy answer. Women who are determined to find an easy way out of their sin are simply wasting precious time groping around for what does not exist. *A life which has become out of control only comes back under control through the processes of God's discipline.*

Biblical Precedents

Since childhood most of us have been bombarded with a lifestyle of instant gratification, selfish indulgence, superficial relationships, and shallow commitments. At some point, those who plan on living a genuine Christian life must come to grips with this un-Christlike way of living and face their need for change. Godly discipline allows a person to live a holy life in the midst of a decadent and perverse society such as ours.

Scripture has much to say about the concept of discipline. *Chastisement, reproof, warning, correction, instruction,* and *training* are all terms used under the general theme of discipline in the Bible. These may not be popular terms in our "anything goes" culture, but collectively they describe the way God deals with His children in all ages.

The Bible clearly expresses that human beings begin life off track spiritually. Solomon, speaking under a powerful anointing of wisdom, repeatedly counseled parents about the need to establish discipline in a child's life at an early age. "Foolishness is bound up in the heart of a child; the rod of discipline will remove it far from him." (Proverbs 22:15) "The rod and reproof give wisdom, but a child who gets his own way brings shame to his mother." (Proverbs 29:15) "Discipline your son while there is hope, and do not desire his death." (Proverbs 19:18) "He who spares his rod hates his son, but he who loves him disciplines him diligently." (Proverbs 13:24)

These are wise words for parents raising children in our day and age. Nevertheless, there is a spiritual truth that is much deeper than the practical truth being expressed here. Children come into a wicked world with a natural inclination toward sin and rebellion to God's prescribed way of living. Just as a baby's nature must be dealt with early on, so too must the new child of God learn about the hand of discipline from a loving, heavenly Father. Ministers who attempt to bypass this important aspect of spiritual growth are poor examples of what a spiritual parent should be. The writer of Hebrews said the following:

> You have not yet resisted to the point of shedding blood in your striving against sin; and you have forgotten the exhortation which is addressed to you as sons, "My son, do not regard lightly the discipline of the Lord, nor faint when you are reproved by Him; for those whom the Lord loves He disciplines, and He scourges every son whom He receives." It is for discipline that you endure; God deals with you as with sons; for what son is there whom his father does not discipline? But if you are without discipline, of which all have become partakers, then you are illegitimate children and not sons. Furthermore, we had earthly fathers to discipline us, and we respected them; shall we not much rather be subject to the Father of spirits, and live? For they disciplined us for a short time as seemed best to them, but He disciplines us for

our good, that we may share His holiness. All discipline for the moment seems not to be joyful, but sorrowful; yet to those who have been trained by it, afterwards it yields the peaceful fruit of righteousness. (Hebrews 12:4-11)

This wonderful passage of Scripture, which follows the great faith chapter of the Bible, presents a basic principle of the Christian life: "If you are without discipline," the writer of Hebrews asserts, "then you are illegitimate children and not sons." Though Christians might try to avoid God's discipline in their lives, if a person is truly a child of God, it is inevitable that he or she will face God's rod of correction. I sincerely question the salvation of those who never seem to face any godly discipline. The following is a letter from Kathy's book, *When His Secret Sin Breaks Your Heart: Letters To Hurting Wives*. It expresses this truth perfectly.

Dear Lucy,

I'm so sorry to hear that your husband ran off with another woman. It must be crushing for you to hear how happy they are, especially since it seems as though everything in your life is crashing down around you. They are both making good money, going to church, living a prosperous life and seemingly without any troubles. How different your life must be. Your job hardly pays you enough to get by. The engine in your car must be rebuilt. You feel very alone. I can understand why you feel like God is blessing them and cursing you.

Lucy, has it occurred to you that these two may not even know the Lord? I realize they claim to be Christians, but their conduct seems anything but Christ-like to me. At the very least, they are terribly backslidden and in real delusion. Everything going well is not necessarily a sign of God's blessing on one's life. In fact, in a case like this especially, it appears to be a *lack* of God's hand on their lives.

Look at your life in comparison. You are a sincere believer, struggling to keep life together in the midst of grief and adversity. I have known much of this in my relationship with God. Allow me to share the words of Solomon with you: "My son, do not reject the discipline of the LORD, or loathe His reproof, for whom the LORD loves He reproves, even as a father, the son in whom he delights." (Proverbs 3:11-12)

I do not know enough about this situation to make any real judgments, but it looks as though your husband and his girlfriend are going their own way, without the slightest genuine concern about what God thinks. You, however, are being refined in the furnace of affliction.

Do not let their outward "happiness" fool you, Lucy. Happiness based upon favorable circumstances is only an inch deep. Solomon said, "…the way of transgressors is hard." (Proverbs 13:15 KJV) One day they will have to deal with the consequences of their actions; whether it be here on earth, or standing before a holy God.

The wonderful news for you is that God loves you enough to be extremely concerned about every aspect of your life. Though it seems He is far away during times like these He has never been closer. Turn to Him for the comfort that only He can give you.

The Reaction to Discipline

Many of us received the instruction Solomon gives in Proverbs 5 but simply refused to heed it:

Now then, my sons, listen to me, and do not depart from the words of my mouth. Keep your way far from [the adulteress], and do not go near the door of her house, lest you give your vigor to others, and your years to the cruel one; lest strangers be filled with your strength, and your hard-earned goods go to the house of an alien; and you groan at your latter end, when your flesh and your body are consumed; and you say, "How I have hated instruction! And my heart spurned reproof! And I have not listened to the voice of my teachers, nor inclined my ear to my instructors!" (Proverbs 5:7-13)

On a rare occasion, a young man will come into the Pure Life Ministries Live-in program seeking help before he throws his life away. However, most Christians who give over to sexual sin will suffer years of consequences before they are willing to allow God to begin a work of correction in their lives.

Sadly, there are also many who will never learn. They are like the man who broke his arm, but was unwilling to go to the doctor. He decided that he would rather live with a lame arm than to go through the pain of having it set. People who have given over to sexual sin are also broken up inside. Most must face the consequences of unhealthy childhoods or suffer the penalty for the poor decisions they have made. Every time the Lord draws close to bring the needed correction, they pull away. They feel that they cannot handle the pain of the reality of what they have been like. The real problem is that they, like the fool of Proverbs, only live life for today. Though the process of discipline would ultimately bring joy and freedom, they cannot see beyond what is easiest at the present moment.

That is why Solomon said, "A rebuke goes deeper into one who has understanding than a hundred blows into a fool." (Proverbs 17:10) He also said, "Though you pound a fool in a mortar with a pestle along with crushed grain, yet his folly will not depart from him." (Proverbs 27:22) There are those who refuse to learn, regardless of the price of their folly. The woman who

Positive			Negative	
Verse	What he does	Result or reality	What he does	Result or reality
10:17	heeds instruction	on the path of life	forsakes reproof	goes astray
12:1	loves discipline	loves knowledge	hates reproof	called stupid
13:1	accepts discipline	called wise	does not listen	called a scoffer
13:18	regards reproof	will be honored	neglects discipline	poverty & shame
15:5	regards reproof	called prudent	rejects discipline	called a fool
15:10			forsakes the way	stern discipline
			hates reproof	will die
15:31	listens to reproof	dwell with wise		
15:32	listens to reproof	acquires understanding	neglects discipline	despises himself
29:1			hardens himself	beyond remedy

Figure 14-1

will not receive instruction from the Lord is destined to repeat the same lessons over and over again. She is like the person described in Proverbs who did not want (1:25), would not accept, spurned (1:30), rejected, loathed (3:11), forsook (10:17), would not listen to (13:1) and even hated (5:12) the instruction of the Lord. Many, who have been this way in the past, are now learning to turn to (1:23), heed (10:17), regard (13:18), listen to (15:31-32), accept (13:1) and even love (12:1) God's reproof.

In Figure 14-1, we see a chart which outlines various verses from the Book of Proverbs regarding those who accept or reject the discipline of the Lord. Hebrew writing style commonly utilizes contrasts, such as good and evil, light and darkness, and/or foolishness and wisdom. In the verses listed, a comparison is given between a person who turns to God's process of correction and of one who turns away from it. From these passages one can readily distinguish between the wise and the foolish.

The Ways of Discipline

God's discipline in the lives of His children is as diverse as the problems He must correct. For example, Peter's life is one which is characterized by a great deal of correction. Do you recall when Jesus asked the disciples who people considered

Him to be? Various notions were expressed; but then Peter, temporarily filled with a word from God, stood up boldly and exclaimed, "Thou art the Christ, the Son of the living God." What a declaration! This was one of those times you wish someone had been running a camcorder for all posterity! It was certainly one of Peter's greatest moments.

Jesus, never one to bypass an opportunity to bless someone, turned to Peter and said, "Blessed are you, Simon Barjona, because flesh and blood did not reveal this to you, but My Father who is in heaven. And I also say to you that you are Peter, and upon this rock I will build My church; and the gates of Hades shall not overpower it. I will give you the keys of the kingdom of heaven; and whatever you shall bind on earth shall be bound in heaven, and whatever you shall loose on earth shall be loosed in heaven."

Wow! How would it make you feel to have the Son of God say something like that to you in front of all your friends? I can just see Peter's head swelling. And, according to the law of gravity, what goes up must come down. A few minutes later, when Jesus disclosed what He would have to endure in Jerusalem, Peter rebuked Him. Imagine that! Peter, overflowing with pride, now thinks he is in a position to rebuke God!

With great authority Jesus whirled around and said to Peter, "Get behind Me, Satan! You are a stumbling block to Me; for you are not setting your mind on God's interests, but man's." (Matthew 16:15-23) I do not understand how a man can be speaking by the word of the Lord one minute and speaking by Satan the next, but so it was. Peter received a piercing rebuke from Jesus. It is important to keep in mind that the Lord was not just venting frustration, as one of us might. His only concern was that Peter would learn to discern the difference between the voice of the Holy Spirit and the voice of the enemy. Peter was taught a lesson that day by the greatest Teacher known to man, and he probably never forgot it.

The Lord may also graciously correct His children through other believers. Paul describes an incident he had with Peter. Paul was facing constant opposition from the Judaisers, Jews who had supposedly converted to Christianity but wanted to retain the law. Peter had stood by Paul in the midst of the conflict. He could clearly see the hand of the Lord in Paul's work. Later, Peter came to Syrian Antioch where Paul's home church was located. Peter fellowshipped freely with the recently converted Gentiles *until* a group of Judaisers showed up from Jerusalem. Suddenly, he distanced himself from the Gentiles, probably making them feel as though they were rejected by the Lord. Paul confronted him publicly. "If you, being a Jew, live like the Gentiles and not like the Jews," the Apostle stormed, "how is it that you compel the Gentiles to live like Jews?" (Galatians 2:14)

Sometimes a sharp rebuke is the very thing we need to get us back on track—to bring us down off our "high horse," so to speak. In this case, Peter's fear of man was exposed for all to see. God could have laid it on Paul's heart to take Peter aside and gently point out how he was being more concerned about what the Judaisers thought of him than he was about the welfare of the Gentiles. However, lessons that will create a restraining wall around a Christian in preparation for future temptations usually come at a tremendous price.

Other lessons are even more painful. Who can forget what Peter experienced the night Jesus was arrested? The Lord was sitting around the table eating the Last Supper with His disciples. He decided it was time to tell them what was to take place that night; He would be betrayed, arrested, and then crucified. The overly-confident Peter could not bear to hear this kind of talk. "Lord, I will lay down my life for You," he said with undeniable self-assurance.

Jesus answered, "Will you lay down your life for Me? Truly, truly, I say to you, a cock shall not crow, until you deny Me three times."

Still full of his false confidence, Peter answered, "Even though all may fall away because of You, I will never fall away…Even if I have to die with You, I will not deny You," (A compilation of Matthew 26 & John 13).

Within a few hours, Peter learned the painful lesson of depending upon one's own strengths and abilities. After he denied Him a third time, Jesus, who happened to be shoved out the door at that very moment, looked at His trusted disciple. One look from those eyes of love was enough to break Peter's heart. We are told that Peter "went out and wept bitterly." (Luke 22:62)

One might wonder why God is so hard on those He loves. I encourage you to spend some time reading the epistles of First and Second Peter. You will read the words of a man who had been through the process of God's correction for over thirty years. Peter did not become a man who God could speak such words of life through simply because he followed Jesus for three years. The life of Judas is clear evidence that just being around Jesus did not, in itself, produce such a life change. Peter had matured and had a deeper revelation of the things of God because he allowed the Lord to correct him over the years. We might also consider the fact that if the Lord felt that a man like Peter needed to be regularly disciplined, how much more so those who are in habitual sin? Again, "For whom the LORD loves He reproves, even as a father, the son in whom he delights." (Proverbs 3:12)

Disciplined for Character

Perhaps you are thinking, "Well, that's fine for Peter. He was one of the disciples. But I'm not going to be writing any books of the Bible, and I really don't want to go through God's discipline. I just want to live a normal life, free from this sin that keeps bringing me to ruin." The problem with this sort of thinking is that the woman who will be loosed from sin must exhibit the character of someone who has indeed been set free. However, such character is not generated spontaneously but must be worked into her by the discipline of the Lord.

Solomon said, "Poverty and shame will come to him who neglects discipline, but he who regards reproof will be honored." (Proverbs 13:18) The Hebrew word for honored is a very interesting term. It literally means to be heavy or weighty but is seldom used in a literal way. "From this figurative usage it is an easy step to the concept of a 'weighty' person in society, someone who is honorable, impressive, worthy of respect."[2] The process of God's discipline will eventually make a believer into "a 'weighty' person in society, an honorable, impressive person who is worthy of respect."

This is almost unimaginable for those bound in sexual sin. Though they may display a confident, even arrogant exterior, deep within them there is much shame and guilt over their hidden life. The more sin a woman gives over to, the more her character will be gutted of anything of real substance.

Some women in sexual sin see their sin as a minor quirk in an otherwise impeccable character. Such thinking is sheer fantasy! A woman's behavior in secret is where character—or the lack of it—is revealed. A woman cannot be compartmentalized. She can only act out of the substance of what she consists of as a woman. Secret sexual sin is not a fluke; it is a direct by-product of a woman's character. Her secret behavior will only change as her character changes. Without a restructuring of her character, the woman is certain to return to her behavior. (II Peter 2:20-22)

Some simply try to create honor for themselves. They believe that if they carry themselves with a lot of confidence, they can make themselves seem honorable to those around them. And indeed, there are many who "judge according to appearance" (John 7:24) and are taken in by these "Christian" deceivers. Jesus discerned this brassy approach with some of those around Him.

And He began speaking a parable to the invited guests when He noticed how they had been picking out the places of honor at the table; saying to them, "When you are invited by someone to a wedding feast, do not take the place of honor, lest someone more distinguished than you may have been invited by him, and he who invited you both shall come and say to you, 'Give place to this man,' and then in disgrace you proceed to occupy the last place. But when you are invited, go and recline at the last place, so that when the one who has invited you comes, he may say to you, 'Friend, move up higher'; then you will have honor in the sight of all who are at the table with you. For everyone who exalts himself shall be humbled, and he who humbles himself shall be exalted." (Luke 14:7-11)

Being a woman of honor does not come about by acting as if one deserves to be treated as such. Substance comes as God builds a person's character. Solomon said, "A man's pride will bring him low, but a humble spirit will obtain honor (or weightiness)." (Proverbs 29:23)

Disciplined for Holiness

The last thing to mention regarding the discipline of the Lord is the holiness that comes forth out of it. Perhaps you remember our passage in Hebrews 12, "…He disciplines us for our good, that we may share His holiness."

God does not discipline a woman because He is angry with her. He does it because He has a purpose in mind for her life. He is looking for holiness. As Leonard Ravenhill once wrote, "[God] is not concerned about our happiness but about our holiness."[2] This is an important word for those women who tend to live by their feelings rather than by faith.

Our friend Peter, who experienced much scourging at the hands of his Heavenly Father, helps us see God's purpose: "As obedient children, do not be conformed to the former lusts which were yours in your ignorance, but like the Holy One who called you, be holy yourselves also in all your behavior; because it is written, "YOU SHALL BE HOLY, FOR I AM HOLY." (I Peter 1:14-16)

Holiness does not come from reading a good book. It does not come about by being in a powerful meeting. Holiness comes by the Lord's purging out of us our love for sin and for self. This process takes time.

*"The Spirit has given us life; he must
also control our lives." (Galatians 5:25 GNB)*

I n Paul's letter to the church in Galatia, he wrote, "…Walk in the Spirit, and ye shall not fulfill the lust of the flesh." (Galatians 5:16 KJV) After dealing with thousands of Christians in sexual sin (including many ministers), we have yet to find any evidence to dispute this statement. A woman can go to psychologists, support groups, or deliverance services. She can be prayed for by a famous evangelist or commit herself to a sexual addiction clinic; but if she wants to overcome habitual sin, she must learn to walk in the Spirit. Since the Bible is truly the inspired Word of God, then this conditional promise becomes one of extreme importance to the woman in habitual sexual sin.

I think we would all agree that the phrase "lust of the flesh" accurately characterizes the nature of sexual sin. A few verses later Paul gives a catalog of "the works of the flesh" which begins with "adultery, fornication, uncleanness, lasciviousness, idolatry." (Galatians 5:19-20a KJV) Sexual sin and idolatry are right at the top of the list. How much more so when sex *is* the idol of a woman's life? It is one thing for a woman to dabble in immorality, but it is another matter when she is a regular worshiper *at the altar of sexual idolatry*. She is spiritually bankrupt and desperately needs a way out. Paul gives the escape route with this inconspicuous formula:

"IF...ye walk in the Spirit, THEN...ye shall not fulfill the lust of the flesh."

This conditional promise is so significant that each phrase must be examined carefully so that the full meaning of what is being expressed may be understood and then applied to one's life.

To Walk in the Flesh

In the Bible, the term *walk* describes a certain way one lives his or her life. In our modern day vernacular the term *lifestyle* would be used. This word is not simply describing the kind of day, or even week, someone is having. It is certainly not referring to someone who feels spiritual on Sunday while being in the flesh the rest of the week. When Paul says to "walk in the Spirit," he is describing an ongoing condition of a person's life. If a woman is living her life "in the Spirit," she will not succumb to the desires of her flesh.

It is amazing how a woman can be in the most despicable sin and really believe that she is close to God. We can safely conclude that if a woman is living her life under the dictates of the flesh she is not walking in the Spirit. In fact, I will go even further to say that if a woman is regularly fulfilling the lusts of the flesh, she is indeed walking in the flesh. Thus, we can use the opposite terminology to say, "If you walk in the flesh, you will fulfill the lusts of the flesh." In Galatians 5, Paul gives a comprehensive definition of what it means to walk in the flesh, "Now the deeds of the flesh are evident, which are: immorality, impurity, sensuality, idolatry, sorcery, enmities, strife, jealousy, outbursts of anger, disputes, dissensions, factions, envying, drunkenness, carousing, and things like these, of which I forewarn you just as I have forewarned you that those who practice such things shall not inherit the kingdom of God." (Galatians 5:19-21)

A tenderhearted woman who reads this passage of Scripture will immediately examine her heart, point by point. "Do I give in to impure thoughts or romantic fantasies? Does the desire for pleasure occupy a strong place in my heart? Do I have any idols in my life? Do I have a problem with my temper? Do I ever feel jealous or envious of other people? How often do I find myself embroiled in disputes with others?" Affirmative responses to these questions are all tell-tale signs of a woman who is not walking in the Spirit. However, the one who quickly scans the list with a superficial glance, claiming to be free of such a lifestyle is only deceiving herself. Likewise, so is the woman who wrangles over every term, trying to avoid the truth of what is being expressed.

Jesus said, "If you abide in My word, then you are truly disciples of Mine; and you shall know the truth, and the truth shall make you free." (John 8:31-32) This is also a conditional promise. The woman who lives out the words of Jesus in her daily life will know the truth when she sees it, and that truth will bring her into further liberty. If a woman is going to experience real freedom, it is imperative that she becomes open and brutally honest with herself.

To Walk in the Spirit

There are many who have an occasional experience with God, feel His presence in a church service, or even see Him at work in their lives, and believe they are walking in the Spirit. To walk in the Spirit means that a person's life is dominated, controlled, and guided by the Holy Spirit. Just as the list of "the deeds of the flesh" defines what it means to be in the flesh, the following list of "the fruit of the Spirit" defines what it means to be in the Spirit.

Paul says, "But the fruit of the Spirit is love, joy, peace, patience, kindness, goodness, faithfulness, gentleness, self-control; against such things there is no law. Now those who belong to Christ Jesus have crucified the flesh with its passions and desires. If we live by the Spirit, let us also walk by the Spirit." (Galatians 5:22-25) Again, the woman who is willing to be honest with herself will examine this list and ask the difficult questions: "Am I really as devoted to the lives of others as I am to myself? Do I have the patience to endure difficult people and trying circumstances without losing the sense of God's presence? How kind am I to those who cross my will? Am I truly living in subjection to the Holy Spirit everyday?"

As the fruit of the Spirit increases in a woman's life, it helps her mature in other areas of her life as well. As a woman grows in faith, she will be strengthened to grow in meekness also. A good gauge for a woman to use to examine where she is spiritually is to examine her weakest point. For addicts, the lack of self-control is a glaring manifestation of a deeply-rooted problem.

If you walk in the Spirit, you will not fulfill the lusts of the flesh. At first glance, one would think the key word in this phrase is either "walk," or "Spirit." However, the primary term we want to focus on here is "in." As considered earlier, just as the spirit of this world creates an atmosphere a woman can abide in, so too does the Spirit of God.* A woman who lives her daily life in an atmosphere of God is not going to give in to or pursue lusts that may still lie dormant within her nature.

The Apostle John said, "And you know that He appeared in order to take away sins; and in Him there is no sin. No one who abides in Him sins; no one who sins has seen Him or knows Him...And the one who keeps His commandments abides in Him, and He in him. And we know by this that He abides in us,

---

* The truth of the matter is that the enemy counterfeits what God does.

by the Spirit whom He has given us." (I John 3:5-6, 24) These verses do not suggest that a person lives in sinless perfection—only that there is no sin which is *ruling* her life. The Spirit and grace of Jesus Christ sustains her at a level above dominating sin. This way of living within the control of the Holy Spirit does not happen overnight; it is developed within a believer's life as she matures.

The Daily Sustenance of Prayer

"The worst thing you can do with [women involved in sexual sin] is lecture them about praying more or asking God for help. They've already done that, often to the point of despair." Such were the blasphemous words of a "Christian" therapist who has made a career out of counseling struggling women. She went on to assert that the only real hope for sexual addiction is found through psychotherapy.

There is no mistaking the inference here: God is not trustworthy. You can cry out to Him until you're blue in the face and nothing is going to happen. Such sentiments are extremely poisonous to one's faith and paralyze the hungry soul from believing God for deliverance. Clearly this woman has no comprehension of what it means to have a real life in God.

The New Testament offers bright hope for the person who learns to truly take refuge in God. Notwithstanding the assertions made by this false teacher, having a solid devotional life is not only one of the most important elements of a victorious life, but it is also the key to walking in the Spirit. Jesus expressed it this way: "I am the true vine, and My Father is the vinedresser...Abide in Me, and I in you. As the branch cannot bear fruit of itself, unless it abides in the vine, so neither can you, unless you abide in Me. I am the vine, you are the branches; he who abides in Me, and I in him, he bears much fruit; for apart from Me you can do nothing." (John 15:1, 4-5)

There are a number of elements involved with entering into this kind of fellowship. First and foremost is prayer. The very essence of the Christian experience is entering into and maintaining an intimate relationship with God. It is for this purpose that we have been saved from our sins. Yet, how few devote themselves to such blessed intimacy. Attending church is important, but our connection to the Vine must be maintained daily. Imagine what it would be like to have a marriage which was based on nothing more than a formal meeting once or twice a week.

Having a time of prayer each day is essential to the life of a believer. Prayer ushers in the life-changing power of the Holy Spirit. Just as God speaks to us through His word, we talk with Him through prayer. Prayer is simply talking to God. One should not be concerned about being eloquent. The Lord is looking for *real* conversation! He is our dearest Friend and that is how the believer should communicate with Him.

Just as it is with any new spiritual habit, developing a prayer life may be difficult initially. It begins by having a firm conviction that prayer is an essential part of the daily life. The woman who sets herself on the course of cultivating a regular devotional time may find that time seems to drag by slowly at first. This will gradually change as the habit takes root. The woman will soon find herself looking forward to her morning devotions. Before long, the length of time dedicated to communing and fellowshipping with God will grow.

There are at least three keys to a successful prayer life. First, a woman must determine what her *style* of prayer will be. Some like to sit in a room where they can feel free to talk to God without concern about anyone else hearing them. Others like to write their prayers, as it helps them keep their thoughts focused on the Lord. Still others find it easiest to concentrate and talk to the Lord while walking. Each woman has to determine for herself what works for her.

Another key element is choosing *when* to pray. If at all possible, it is always best to pray in the morning. The Lord should get the first fruits of the day. Most people set their alarms only to allow themselves just enough time to get ready for work. The believer who is serious about developing a time with God will begin the routine of early to bed, early to rise. Trying to cram prayer time into an already hectic morning schedule will never work. It will soon fall by the wayside.

The last thing that must be considered is how much time to spend in prayer. Basically, the more time spent with the Lord, the better. What is spoken to God is not as important as just being with Him. Relationships are not established merely on words alone; they are also built on nonverbal communication. God longs to spend time with those He loves. As we have already mentioned, building a devotional life is not easy. The woman who is just beginning to develop a prayer life should avoid overburdening herself. It is much better to be faithful with ten minutes a day than to sporadically spend an hour at a time. The habit is never established in the woman's life who is inconsistent. Until prayer is a regular part of her daily routine, it will always be a drudgery. Once it has become grounded as a consistent element at the start of each day, it becomes effortless. It becomes a good habit!

As the woman begins this new adventure, it is also important that she does not make the mistake of watching a clock; time will appear to slow down. Those who are sitting in a room should turn the clock around so that it cannot be seen. Some might want to set their wrist watch (or even a cooking timer outside the room) which will inform them that their time is up.

As this daily routine becomes a part of the woman's life, she will soon discover that it is no longer a chore to pray. In fact, she will soon find that ten minutes goes by too quickly, and that she will need to pray for fifteen minutes in order to cover all her concerns. As this important spiritual discipline is established, God will begin to give her a burden for the souls of those around her. At this point her prayer life begins to enter into a new phase. She is penetrating the powerful realm of intercession.

As the woman's devotional life progresses, she will also begin to spend more time worshiping the Lord. This is an integral part of growing in our love for God. Some people worship while listening to Christian music they enjoy. However, it is important to remember that simply singing songs that one enjoys is not the same as truly entering into the spirit of worship. Jesus said, "But an hour is coming, and now is, when the true worshipers shall worship the Father in spirit and truth; for such people the Father seeks to be His worshipers. God is spirit, and those who worship Him must worship in spirit and truth." (John 4:23-24) If the woman is truly worshiping God, there is something flowing from her heart toward the Lord. This is what Jesus meant when He talked of worshiping "in spirit and truth." However, there are groups such as Vineyard, Hillsong, Maranatha, and Hosanna which seem to have a real anointing for praise and worship. Some people can benefit greatly by spending time being immersed in this type of Christian music.

Food for the Soul

Spending time in prayer and worship helps the believer to live in the presence of the Holy Spirit each day. There is another aspect to our spiritual equation which is equally important. The Word of God is the source of the believer's spiritual sustenance. It has the inherent power to impute life into a saint's being. A Christian woman needs God's nourishment regularly lest she "dry up." (John 15:6) One problem people in sexual sin face is that their thinking has been warped by the enemy. Think of it as a company spy who broke into the computer room of his chief competitor and messed up the circuitry in their main frame computer. This is a picture of what the devil has done to women who have gotten involved in sexual sin. The enemy has fouled up their inner circuits in such a way that nothing inside them works as it should. Nevertheless, the Word of God has the power to transform a woman from the inside out. Over a period of time, the Word will gradually rewire her circuits if she remains faithful and spends time in the Bible every day.

James spoke of looking "intently at the perfect law." (James 1:25) The Bible deserves our most devoted interest. There are different ways to approach Scripture. Some people like to read vast sections of the Bible at a time. Perhaps they have a system for reading the entire Bible through in a year. However, those who do so should take note that the Word will not penetrate the heart of someone who "speed reads" it.

What typically works better is to study the Bible verse by verse, chapter by chapter, and book by book. This can be accomplished by taking a chapter at a time, reading it with different translations, studying key words, and reading what commentators have to say about that chapter.

Someone else might prefer to "meditate" on Scripture by taking sections of Scripture and carefully mulling over every word. This involves reading those particular sections repeatedly, asking the Holy Spirit to bring the Word "alive" to him. This is often how God reveals precious nuggets of truth to His followers. Dr. Jenson discusses what this approach did in his own life:

> The new habit pattern that had gradually developed in me was not like any other. To become "transformed by the renewing of your mind" (Rom. 12:2) means getting God's Word on the inside to saturate our lives, thoughts, attitudes, emotions, and actions, so that we are conformed from the inside out into the likeness of Jesus Christ.

I am convinced that I had to go through that biblical process of meditation just as I had meditated on lewd pictures and thoughts for years, building them into my system. The only way to counteract that was to be transformed by the actual renewing of my mind—by meditating on the Word of God...[1]

We cannot emphasize enough the importance of soaking up God's Word. The woman may not be changed overnight, but the change will come in time. As we have said to struggling Christians in the past, "If you don't want to be in the same condition two months from now, you better get right on it! Every day that you prolong starting is that much longer that you will be going through this suffering."

As long term, effectual changes occur within you through the Word, spending time in the presence of God daily will help you to "walk in the Spirit." Thus, both your mind and heart will be transformed by the power of God.

CHAPTER SIXTEEN:
OVERCOMING LUST

*"Therefore do not let sin reign in your mortal body
so that you obey its lusts." (Romans 6:12)*

The woman who has become addicted to (reactive and/or proactive) lust can and must overcome it. But lust will not just disappear. The woman who is serious about walking in purity must be willing to take some drastic measures. There are three aspects to lust which she will have to address. Providentially, each of these elements carries with it a weapon with which to attack the problem.

Conditions Conducive to Lust

The spirit of this world creates spiritual atmospheres conducive to lust. The Apostle John said, "Do not love the world, nor the things in the world. If anyone loves the world, the love of the Father is not in him. For all that is in the world, the lust of the flesh and the lust of the eyes and the boastful pride of life, is not from the Father, but is from the world. And the world is passing away, and also its lusts; but the one who does the will of God abides forever." (I John 2:15-17)

The world is full of lust. In practical terms, the spirit of this world capitalizes upon the fact that humans have carnal desires which are innate within them: the lust for pleasure, the lust for gain, and the lust for position. The enemy constantly attempts to create certain atmospheres which are tailor-made for the particular lust within us. Hence, the devil is called "the prince of the power of the air." For instance, if one were to go to a mall, she would find an atmosphere there which promotes covetousness. Women especially are vulnerable to the displays in the clothing stores. There is a pervasive spiritual climate in the mall which provokes people to want more and more and more. Beauty salons are notorious for their carnal atmospheres. It seems that the conversation typically either revolves around sharing gossip or discussing worldly interests. If a woman goes into a bar, the ambience puts her in a partying mood. Nevertheless, it is the enemy at work in each of these settings.

For women struggling with romantic fantasies or sexual sin, there must be a constant awareness of the atmospheres which tend to provoke lust. For instance, it is not advisable for such a woman to spend time browsing at a magazine rack. The fare offered in such places is very conducive to carnal thinking.

Even the home must be carefully guarded. Television, as we have already discussed, is a way the enemy can bring a lustful atmosphere right into your living room. The best approach is to get rid of it or, at least, eliminate broadcast and satellite connections. By limiting herself to using DVD's, the woman can be very selective about what is watched in the home.

Frequently, the Internet is also a trap of the enemy. Pornography sites on the web are the most-frequented sites, and are by far the largest money-makers through Internet commerce. For the woman who has broken the barrier and has accessed Internet pornography, merely sitting down at a computer to perform legitimate tasks can replicate a familiar atmosphere that quickly provokes serious temptation. For this reason, and because filters are not fail-proof, terminating access to the Internet entirely may be an essential step.

It is important to ruthlessly root out anything in the home which the devil might use in a time of weakness. The woman who is going to get the victory over lust must do everything within her power to minimize the enemy's ability to affect her spiritually.

Quenching the Flames of Hell

Who can adequately describe the hell of living in the spirit of lust? To be driven with a whip but never satisfied...to commit humiliating and degrading acts...to strive with all one's heart for some experience and then once it has been accomplished, find it to be empty and unsatisfying...to have one's thinking become dark, evil, and even insane...to hurt loved ones again and again...to experience a life of misery, despair, and hopelessness...to find oneself drifting further and further away from God...Anyone who has lived this kind of life knows more about the flames of hell than he or she may realize.

Lustful living is hellish living. Again, lust is demanding and never satisfied. The more one feeds the beast, the more ravenous it becomes. Perhaps the allergic reaction to poison ivy would illustrate the intense craving for immorality some are consumed by. The body becomes covered with a rash which incites intense itching. If the woman scratches the infected area, she risks the possibility of making it worse and spreading it to other parts of her body. If she does not scratch it, she feels as though she might go insane! Yet, even if she grated it with a metal file, a few minutes later it would itch all the more.

One of the keys to bringing one's mind into subjection to the Spirit is that of learning to be thankful. *Gratitude quenches the fire of lust.* A thankful spirit destroys the driving passion for sex and romance because it creates contentment within the woman's heart. It soothes the beast, smothers the flames, and medicates the itch. The message behind lust is, "I want! I want! I want!"

The feeling lodged within the grateful heart is, "Look at all I have! Thank You Lord, for all that You have done for me and given me. I don't need anything else." A grateful heart is a full heart. When a woman is content with life, she will not be driven by the lust for what she should not have.

There are those who would say, "What do I have to be grateful for? My life is nothing but a total mess. I am absolutely miserable. I feel pressured to quit habits that I can't seem to quit. I'm not happy in the world, but I'm also not happy as a Christian. What exactly do I have to be grateful for?" It has never occurred to them that a large part of the reason they are in such a predicament is because of their unthankful, stingy spirit. What a different outlook than that of the little old lady living in poverty who looked down at the scrap of dry bread and cup of water sitting on the table in front of her and exclaimed, "What, all this and Christ too?!"

It brings to mind the story of two little boys, both nine years old. Johnny's daddy is an affluent attorney in a big city. At Christmas time he purchased his son a large number of gifts. The one he was most excited about was the Nintendo Game Cube he bought for his boy. On Christmas Eve, he was careful to put it all the way in the back of the tree so that it would be the last present Johnny would open. The following morning the nine-year-old impatiently opened and tossed aside all his presents. His dad's anticipation was mounting as Johnny finally grabbed the last package. He tore off the wrapping paper, discovered the Nintendo, and threw it down. "I wanted a Sony Playstation!" he yelled, storming off to his bedroom, slamming the door behind him.

Meanwhile, down in the heart of Mexico there is an orphanage where unwanted little boys and girls are abandoned. Life in the dilapidated facility is all that little Juan has ever known. On this same Christmas morning, an American pastor showed up with a truckload of used toys he had collected at the church. He began handing out assorted toys to all the children. He could not help but notice Juan standing off to the side. He went into the truck and pulled out a bike: broken spokes, bent handle-bars and all. Wheeling it down the ramp to Juan, he said, "Here little guy, this is for you." The little boy looked up at him in amazement. Nobody had ever given him anything. He could not believe it. "Go ahead, Juan. It's for you." At that, the timid youngster jumped on the bike and began riding around the parking lot laughing and crying with joy.

These two boys represent the attitudes we can choose to have in life. We have so much to be grateful for in America. God has truly shed His grace upon our country. Much more important than the outward prosperity we enjoy is all that God has done for us as believers. A quick breeze through Scripture reveals just a few things which God gives His children. He parted with His Son, the most precious gift He had to offer, to die on the cross for us. (John 3:16) He bestows eternal life, (Romans 6:23) and gives all things pertaining to life and godliness. (II Peter 1:3) He hands us the keys to the kingdom, (Matthew 16:19) and bestows upon us the power to tread upon serpents. (Luke 10:19) He distributes spiritual gifts. (I Corinthians 12) He imparts to us the power to become children of God. (John 1:12) He gives us a Spirit of power, of love and of a sound mind. (II Timothy 1:7) He makes it possible for us to have victory through Jesus. (I Corinthians 15:57) He provides us with all of the wisdom we need. (James 1:5) He gives us the Holy Spirit. (Acts 2:38) For Christians, there is no limit to our gratitude lists. If a believer is not grateful it is because he or she willfully chooses not to be.

Gratitude is a disposition of the heart that must be encouraged and nurtured. If a woman waits until she feels like being thankful, it might never happen. She must make it a priority to develop a habit of being grateful regardless of her circumstances. There are two basic things one can do which will help. First, the woman needs to repent of complaining.

This means she asks the Lord to forgive her for her spirit of ingratitude. She must make a commitment to quit grumbling. She will have to repent of self-pity because it is the underlying disposition which fosters thanklessness. She must also repent of being demanding and selfish in life. Christians should strive to be in the spirit Juan was in, rather than the attitude Johnny displayed.

Secondly, she must learn to start expressing gratitude. She should regularly thank the Lord for all that He has done in her life. God has certainly been extremely patient with those of us who have struggled with sexual sin. We have much to be thankful for! Another practical exercise one can do is to make gratitude lists. For instance, a woman can make a list of all the things she can think of that she is grateful for in life. Perhaps the following week she will make one about her job, or husband, pastor or kids.

Doing gratitude lists will have an unbelievable effect on the spirit a woman is in. For those who are especially ungrateful, perhaps they should go to the local video store and rent *A Christmas Carol*! The message of that movie is certainly appropriate to the miserable woman who is never satisfied with life and cannot find anything to thank God for.

Part of the problem with women involved in habitual sexual sin is that they have lived in the fast lane of sexual experiences for so long they can hardly handle the slow lane and doing the speed limit. If a woman is accustomed to driving 80 m.p.h., 55 seems like a snail's speed. It drives the flesh crazy. However, if she will get in the slow lane and force herself to stay there, the frenzy she feels inside will eventually subside, and 55 m.p.h. will seem fast!

The problem with trying to live life at 80 m.p.h. is that no one can maintain that level. Life was not meant to be lived at such a pace. Figure 16-1, on the next page, shows the life of the typical sexual addict. She is unwilling to live in the 40-60 m.p.h. range

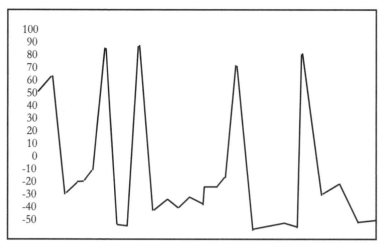

Figure 16-1

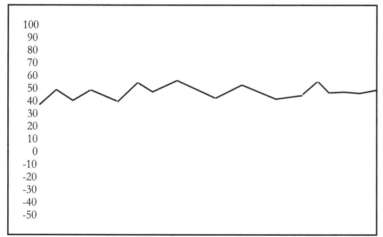

Figure 16-2

with everyone else. She is continually trying to enhance her life with new romantic fantasies or exciting sexual experiences. Since there is such a price with sin, once she has culminated her lust, she plummets into the depths of despair and hopelessness. She believes the only way to escape depression is to boost herself up with a new romantic or sexual experience.

Figure 16-2, on the previous page, shows the life of a woman who is content with her life in God. Her life is not characterized by extreme peaks and valleys. Since she does not experience the despair of sin, she does not feel a need to pump herself up with the false high of illicit sex. She is content to live her life at 50 m.p.h. What is wrong with that? If God can make her satisfied with Him, wouldn't that be better than trying to live at a pace she was not created for? This seems unattainable to some but only because they are accustomed to living life by their feelings rather than by faith.

Cleansing the Cup

In the seventh chapter we discussed the need to pull down the façades of holiness and to expose the true nature of one's heart. This same terminology is used by Jesus when speaking about the Pharisees. One day He was eating with the Pharisees when one of them criticized Him for not ceremonially washing His hands before eating. This would be comparable to a Christian not bowing his head and making a show of saying grace before dinner. Jesus turned to them and said, "Now you Pharisees clean the outside of the cup and of the platter; but inside of you, you are full of robbery and wickedness. You foolish ones, did not He who made the outside make the inside also? But give that which is within as charity, and then all things are clean for you." (Luke 11:39-41)

We have dealt with thousands of Christians in sexual sin since 1986. Many had learned to clean the outward life. They faithfully attended church. They quit their past life of partying and carousing. They had repented of the open rebellion they had once lived in toward God. Outwardly they seemed to be doing fairly well. However, it was another matter inwardly. Although they had cleaned the outside of the cup, their inside world was still full of wickedness, and, as the Lord said of the Pharisees on another occasion, "self-indulgence." (Matthew 23:25)

Jesus did not scold the Pharisees for cleaning up their outward lives. It is pleasing to God for us to go to church and to repent of that outward visible evidence of wickedness. He was trying to teach them that it is just as important to cleanse the inside life as well. Many women who have been controlled by a driving lust have managed to overcome the outward acts of sexual sin, but are still consumed by lust inside. Something must change in the inward life.

Jesus gave the answer to the Pharisees that day. "...*give that which is within as charity, and then all things are clean for you.*" In that one word He put His finger right on the problem. In their hearts the Pharisees were not *givers* but *takers*. How opposite was our Savior! He spent His entire ministry doing for others. His life was one devoted to doing acts of mercy. He constantly sacrificed for the sake of others, always showing kindness, healing, delivering, teaching, and *giving*. What was within Him came out in the form of mercy, love, and compassion.

In that one word, *giving*, He provides the answer to the woman who has learned how to do the outward things of religion and yet is still filled with wicked thinking. This one word, which is used some two thousand times in Scripture, describes the fundamental nature of God, and consequently what it means to be godly. It also describes why many remain defeated. The steps outlined in this book will lead the struggling woman toward victory. She can close the avenues she has opened up to the devil. She can allow God to deal with her flesh and go through His mighty process of discipline. She can avoid the schemes of the enemy. She can see what she is like and go through a real breaking over it. She can develop a wonderful devotional life. However, if she is going to be cleansed on the inside, a transformation will have to take place within. She must take less and give more!

The Prison of Self

In Chapter Six we compared sexual addiction to bedsores, saying that until the woman is cured of the medical ailment that is keeping her bedridden, she will never rid herself of the sores. We wrote, "...sexual addiction is a by-product of a self-centered lifestyle. The woman is addicted to illicit sex *because* she is consumed with SELF."

A woman's self-life and addiction are inextricably tied together. The two strengthen each other. The stronger the self-life, the more virulent will be the addiction. Likewise, the more she gives over to her beloved sin, the more self-centered she becomes.

Genuine Christianity, however, breaks down the self-life and sets a person free. The process of brokenness and repentance discussed in Chapter Thirteen describes what happens when a person's hard shell of self is delivered a powerful blow. It makes a way for the Spirit of Jesus to come into the person's heart and reign as king.

Many people consider themselves to be Christians simply because there has been a legitimate alteration in their lifestyles to accommodate the unspoken list of rules that is part of the prevailing mindset of modern Evangelicalism. Although the person has renounced a few bad habits and has incorporated church into her life, self remains lodged on the throne of the heart. Her life is still controlled by a lust for what this world offers.

But the Christianity of the New Testament is something much deeper than mere outward religion. An authentic convert has repented of her rebellion to God's rule and has put her faith in Christ. Love becomes the dominant characteristic of the woman's life who truly has Jesus abiding within. In fact, the Apostle John gave this as one of the evidences of whether or not a person has truly been born again. He wrote, "We know that we have passed out of death into life, because we love the brethren. He who does not love abides in death." (I John 3:14) Years earlier Jesus had said, "By this all men will know that you are My disciples, if you have love for one another." (John 13:35)

Obviously, we don't do acts of love to save ourselves, but the woman who has truly come into real Christianity will find that she now has the spiritual wherewithal to love others. She must now act upon that new abiding principle.

Most Christians we have dealt with over the years think they do love other people. But the love of God means much more than simply being a nice person.* In simplest terms, love means to give of oneself.

Jesus said, "...give that which is within as charity, and then all things are clean for you." As the woman learns to become a giver in her heart, she will begin to view everything in life differently. She will be cleansed inside. For the woman who has lived her entire life in self-centeredness, this concept seems completely foreign. "Look, I just want to get rid of this fantasy problem. I'm not looking to turn the world upside-down." Yet, this is the answer that Jesus gave to those who needed a great inner purging. He said to give. It is the opposite spirit of wanting to take for self.

Jesus said, "Heal the sick, raise the dead, cleanse the lepers, cast out demons; freely you received, freely give." (Matthew 10:8) In other words, go out and meet the needs of others. Someone once said that lust is seeing people as Satan sees them; but we need to see others as God sees them. As you do this, the Lord's compassion will begin to grow within you. A gradual change will occur in your heart. Rather than seeing people as objects to use for your own selfish purposes, you will begin to see them as people with problems, struggles, and hurts. You will begin to invest your life in theirs for *their* good. This is

---

* Can we remind the reader that the unregenerate world and hell itself are both full of "nice" people? Jesus said, "If you love those who love you, what credit is *that* to you? For even sinners love those who love them." (Luke 6:32)

the normal Christian life. Anyone can claim to be a follower of Christ, but those who truly have the Spirit of God within them will eventually be compelled to love other people. Oswald Chambers said:

> When the Holy Spirit has shed abroad the love of God in our hearts, then that love requires cultivation. No love on earth will develop without being cultivated. We have to dedicate ourselves to love, which means identifying ourselves with God's interests in other people.[1]

With regard to sin, Jesus taught that, "All these evil things proceed from within and defile the man." (Mark 7:23) If the sin is in the heart, would not the best place to deal with it be in the heart? Jesus also said to give that which is within. The key, then, is to turn one's heart into one of goodness. The best way to accomplish this is by praying for others. As the woman learns to truly intercede for the needs of other people, a transformation will occur. She will become a giver in her heart instead of a taker. God wants a spirit of blessing to be within His people all the time. The more a woman prays for others, the less she will become irritated, offended and provoked by them; and yes, the less they will appeal to her romantically or sexually.

Praying for others is definitely a huge step in the right direction. The change will soon break out of the heart into outward actions. The old stinginess will be replaced with a new spirit of giving. Just like the transformation ole' Scrooge went through, the woman will soon be looking for opportunities to meet needs. She will delight in giving her time, money, and possessions. More importantly, she will give her life away: just so others may prosper and be blessed. Certainly what Jesus said is true: "It is more blessed to give than to receive." (Acts 20:35)

The possibilities of getting involved in the needs of others are limitless. Nursing home ministries are always looking for volunteers to help the elderly who have often been forgotten and abandoned by family and friends. What a wonderful place to live out the mercy which God has shown to you. Jail ministries need women who will take an interest in those behind bars. Girls need Sunday school teachers who will take an interest in their lives; and soup kitchens need people who will come out and serve unselfishly. If nothing else, one can go to her pastor and offer to serve in whatever capacity is necessary to help the ministry. Most pastors are inundated with pastoral obligations and various problems concerning members of their congregation and have very few people willing to give of their time.

It is very important that one does not get into situations which will bring glory to one's self. Women who have been involved in sexual sin must first learn to become *servants*. To become involved in a leadership position where one is noticed by others will defeat the entire purpose. Jesus said, "Beware of practicing your righteousness before men to be noticed by them; otherwise you have no reward with your Father who is in heaven." (Matthew 6:1) *A woman has to unselfishly serve or nothing will change inside her.*

If the woman will get out of herself, she will soon come to understand the blessed life of being a giver. There is not a devil in hell that can stop her from living out God's love to other people. Until she begins to do this, she will remain imprisoned behind the walls of her own selfishness.

Close every avenue the enemy might have to affect your soul; develop and nurture a thankful spirit; and learn to be a giver instead of a taker. These spiritual exercises will transform the way you see other people; you will begin to see them through the eyes of the One who laid down His life for both you and them.

"Grace instructs us to give up ungodly living and
worldly passions, and to live self-controlled,
upright, and godly lives in this world."
(Titus 2:12 GNB)

When the Pharisees were ready to stone the woman to death who was caught in adultery in John 8, they *did* have legal precedence. Old Testament law could not be clearer: "If *there is* a man who commits adultery with another man's wife, one who commits adultery with his friend's wife, the adulterer and the adulteress shall surely be put to death." (Leviticus 20:10) The punishment was clearly stated. There were no misunderstandings, nor any exceptions.

Those of us who have only known the dispensation of grace must continually face the temptation to disregard God's judicial system in our lives. "That doesn't apply to us anymore," one might say, "we are not under the law." Yes, that is true. Nevertheless, "the law," Paul tells us, "has become our tutor to lead us to Christ." (Galatians 3:24) In other words, coming to an understanding of how God views sin will lead us into a revelation of Jesus Christ. God sending His Son to die a cruel, horrible death on the Cross does not mean He no longer hates sin and has disregarded His judicial system. It simply means that His Son's death provided an atonement for our sin. We are no longer required to pay the full penalty for our transgressions. God now only requires that we confess our sins and repent of them. His grace means that those of us who have lived disobedient lives should now dwell in the grateful awareness that we are criminals who deserve the death penalty, but have been given a pardon because the Judge ordered His Son to suffer the punishment on our behalf.

Unfortunately, a sinister and flippant attitude has crept into the Church. Our perspective of the horrible nature of sin has become so distorted by humanism that if God dealt with a man or woman today as He did with those during Old Testament times, we would feel that He had been too harsh and unmerciful. If a modern day Ananias and Sapphira were struck dead by our holy God, we would literally become unraveled. By and large the Church is quite comfortable with the very thing that this holy Being hates: SIN.

Grace Is Not a Synonym for Patience

One day, high up on the lonely crags of Mt. Sinai, God revealed Himself to Moses. As He passed in front of the old prophet, He proclaimed, "The LORD, the LORD God, compassionate and gracious, slow to anger, and abounding in lovingkindness and truth; who keeps lovingkindness for thousands, who forgives iniquity, transgression and sin; yet He will by no means leave the guilty unpunished, visiting the iniquity of fathers on the children and on the grandchildren to the third and fourth generations." (Exodus 34:6-7) One could easily spend a lifetime studying this self-portrait painted by the Lord and never exhaust its full meaning.

The phrase which holds a special interest to the woman in habitual sin is "slow to anger." Eight times this description is repeated in the Old Covenant about the Lord. Its New Testament equivalent, *makrothumeo,* is translated loosely as patient or longsuffering. This Greek term is used to describe one of the fruits of the Spirit. *Vine's Expository Dictionary* says the following of this term: "...to be patient, longsuffering, to bear with... 'Longsuffering is that quality of self-restraint in the face of provocation which does not hastily retaliate or promptly punish; it is the opposite of anger, and is associated with mercy...'"[1]

For the woman who has continually flouted God's commandments, it is "good news" indeed to find out that He does not get easily angered over her transgressions. In describing this word, *makrothumeo*, Matthew Henry captured the essence of God's heart: "It can endure evil and provocation without being filled with resentment or revenge. It will put up with many slights from the person it loves, and wait long to see the kindly effects of such patience on him."[2]

It is unquestionable that God exhibits tremendous patience towards our open rebellion to His commandments. Nonetheless, we must understand that even though God is patient there will most assuredly be a season of reaping for one's past indiscretions. God's patience should never be confused with His grace. Although they work together, they are two different aspects of His character.

The *Theological Dictionary of the New Testament* says the following about *makrothumeo*: "The majestic God graciously restrains his righteous wrath, as in his saving work for Israel...He does so in covenant faithfulness but also out of regard for human frailty...Forbearance, of course, is not renunciation but postponement with a view to repentance."[3]

God is patient in regard to a woman's sin, but *His patience is for the purpose of giving her time to repent*. Regarding the second coming of the Lord, the Apostle Peter said, "The Lord is not slow about His promise, as some count slowness, but is patient toward you, not wishing for any to perish but for all to come to repentance. But the day of the Lord *will* come." (II Peter 3:9-10a) He then went on to say, "Therefore, beloved,

since you look for these things, be diligent to be found by Him
in peace, spotless and blameless, and regard the patience of our
Lord to be salvation." (II Peter 3:14-15a)

It is extremely dangerous for a woman involved in habitual
sin to assume that because she has not yet had her "day of
reckoning" for her misconduct that there will be no forthcoming
judgment to face.

Grace Is Not a Synonym for Love

Love is a biblical term used to describe the Lord which often
becomes blurred in the minds of believers. God is love, and
the depth, the height, and breadth of His love is immeasurable.
We will limit what we have to say about it to one great, two-
fold truth: God is in a passion to demonstrate His love to us,
and He expects love to be returned to Him.* Jesus said that the
greatest commandment God gave to us was that we love Him
with all our heart, soul and mind. (Matthew 22:37-38) The entire
Bible rests upon this divine mandate.

However, love is not the same as grace. They are two distinct
concepts. Allow us to illustrate the difference between love and
grace with a story from the life of Jesus. He was walking along
one day when a wealthy, young man asked Him what he must do
to be saved. Imagine the penetrating eyes of our Savior bearing
into your inmost being! Mark records the story:

"You know the commandments, do not murder,
do not commit adultery, do not steal, do not bear false
witness, do not defraud, honor your father and mother.
And he said to Him, "Teacher, I have kept all these

---

* The Lord expects us to return His love, but He is not like the selfish person who will
not love another unless his love is returned. God's love is unselfish, giving, and sacrificial
in nature. However, God's love is a lot like electricity; there must be a circuit for it to
be complete. He loves people tremendously, but if that love is not returned, it will
eventually be taken back.

things from my youth up." And looking at him, Jesus felt a love for him, and said to him, "One thing you lack: go and sell all you possess, and give to the poor, and you shall have treasure in heaven; and come, follow Me." But at these words his face fell, and he went away grieved, for he was one who owned much property. And Jesus, looking around, said to His disciples, "How hard it will be for those who are wealthy to enter the kingdom of God!" (Mark 10:19-23)

Many Christians have had awesome experiences in which the love of God became so real that it was almost tangible. Sometimes a worship service can seem as though God's presence can be felt washing over the congregation as gentle waves upon a seashore. The Lord has an enormous love for people. However, one must be careful not to confuse His love with His grace. God's love for mankind is a powerful force. It is easy to get carried away with the feelings produced by that love and to corrupt it into something it is not meant to be. His love does not negate His commandments; He will not simply overlook sin. In fact, if anything, His love demands that we obey Him and turn away from our sin. After the encounter with the rich young ruler, Jesus said to His disciples:

"If anyone loves Me, he will keep My word; and My Father will love him, and We will come to him, and make Our abode with him. He who does not love Me does not keep My words; and the word which you hear is not Mine, but the Father's who sent Me." (John 14:23-24)

The dangerous thing about savoring God's love while in a state of unrepentant sin is that a woman can actually be deceived, thinking she is in true fellowship with the Lord. Notice in the story concerning the rich, young ruler that Jesus' love did not determine this man's eternal destiny. Yes, Mark tells us that Jesus did indeed love him. Undoubtedly, His love manifested itself as a powerful passion which emanated from His very Being. Nonetheless, this man's eternity depended upon *his response* to that ardent love. Would he obey the words of Jesus or not? As Jesus is faithful to do with all those who express a desire to follow Him, He mercifully brought this man to a crossroad—Choose today whom you will serve, God or mammon!

This story is not meant to be a command to give all of one's possessions away. Jesus saw the idolatry in this man's heart, and therefore, He brought him to a fork in the road: If you wish to be My follower, you must forfeit your "idol." We ask you, has the Lord changed? If He laid down this condition to a man regarding money, how much more so those who have made sin their idol?

You will notice also, that once this man made his decision, Jesus did not (as so many Christian leaders today might do) run after him trying to work out some kind of compromise: "Listen, uh, I didn't mean to come on quite so strongly. You probably just need some time to work up to this kind of a commitment. Why don't you follow Me for awhile and hopefully later you can give away some of your money. After all, nobody is perfect. We are all sinners saved by grace. God understands."

Grace Is Not a Synonym for Licentiousness

Jesus continually compelled His followers to respond to His words (i.e. make a decision). He was not content to allow them to follow Him outwardly while not making a real surrender inwardly. He saw right into the core of men's hearts and confronted them about their attitudes.

Jesus not only disregarded the social protocol that one finds in today's "user friendly" churches, but He was actually a stumbling block to many of those who claimed to be His followers. Take, for instance, the major "social blunder" He made, as described in the sixth chapter of John's gospel. The incident began on a very promising note. Jesus fed five thousand people with only two fish and five loaves of bread. The people were so astonished that one even exclaimed, "This is of a truth the Prophet who is to come into the world." (John 6:14) He openly acknowledged what others were afraid to say, that Jesus was the Messiah.

Surely this was a crowd ripe for a tremendous revival service! They were (literally) eating out of His hand. Yet, after that, it was as if He could not say anything right. He began by claiming to be the "bread of heaven." Now, surely He could see that these people needed to be gradually led up to a grand statement such as this. After all, claiming to be the "bread of heaven" to a crowd of simple, country folk was extremely risky. Then, to make matters worse, He went on to tell them that if they wanted to have eternal life they would have to eat His flesh and drink His blood! John tells us that "as a result of this many of His disciples withdrew, and were not walking with Him anymore." (John 6:66) The interesting element to this story is what happened next. Not at all intimidated by the crowd's response, He turned around to His twelve disciples and asked them, "You do not want to go away also, do you?" Simon Peter answered Him, "Lord, to whom shall we go? You have words of eternal life. And we have believed and have come to know that You are the Holy One of God." (John 6:67-68)

Unlike many preachers today who are obsessed with having an enormous congregation, Jesus was interested in those who would pursue Him regardless of the cost. He understood that most would not follow Him, yet He never tempered the piercing truth of God's Word. He loved those people, but He refused to submit a compromised version of what God was offering to all sinners.

This uncompromising stance was maintained by His disciples over the next thirty years. In spite of this, others, whose teachings were characterized by a weak position on sin, came into prominence in the Church. Jude, speaking in the fire of God's Spirit, warned the body of Christ to beware of those "who turn the grace of our God into licentiousness." (Jude 1:4).

We are convinced that what many people today are accepting as grace is really nothing more than *the presumptuous license to sin.* In a book written primarily to those who are continuing to wallow in a lifestyle of ongoing, flagrant sin, it is very important to touch on what the Bible teaches about this matter of grace. Be assured, this is not a discussion involving the age-old argument about the preservation of the saints. It concerns the clear scriptural mandate as to what it means to be a true follower of Christ. John MacArthur, a staunch advocate for the doctrine known as "eternal security," said the following:

> The contemporary church has the idea that salvation is only the granting of eternal life, not necessarily the liberation of a sinner from the bondage of his iniquity. We tell people that God loves them and has a wonderful plan for their lives, but that is only half the truth. God also hates sin and will punish unrepentant sinners with eternal torment. No gospel presentation is complete if it avoids or conceals those facts. Any message that fails to define and confront the severity of personal sin is a deficient gospel. And any "salvation" that does not alter a life-style of sin and transform the heart of the sinner is not a genuine salvation.[4]

Whether you believe that unrepentant sinners have never had a true conversion, or you simply believe that they are backslidden, what the New Testament teaches about the eternal destiny of those who die in habitual sin is exceedingly clear and absolutely irrefutable. In order that you fully understand the penalty for ANY sinner who WILL NOT REPENT and turn from her sin, let us examine the following statements made by Jesus and other God-inspired writers. In no way is this meant to be a "scare tactic," but rather it will hopefully serve as a sobering reminder to all of us how God views sin and the judgment that will fall upon all those who die in their sins.

Jesus spoke these words in the Sermon on the Mount:

"...but I say to you, that everyone who looks on a woman to lust for her has committed adultery with her already in his heart. And if your right eye makes you stumble, tear it out, and throw it from you; for it is better for you that one of the parts of your body perish, than for your whole body to be thrown into hell." (Matthew 5:28-29)

Paul told the Galatians:

"Now the deeds of the flesh are evident, which are: immorality, impurity, sensuality, idolatry...of which I forewarn you just as I have forewarned you that those who practice such things shall not inherit the kingdom of God." (Galatians 5:19-21)

He also warned the church at Corinth:

"Or do you not know that the unrighteous shall not inherit the kingdom of God? Do not be deceived; neither fornicators, nor idolaters, nor adulterers, nor effeminate, nor homosexuals, nor thieves, nor the covetous, nor drunkards, nor revilers, nor swindlers, shall inherit the kingdom of God." (I Corinthians 6:9-10)

The writer of Hebrews said:

"For if we go on sinning willfully after receiving the knowledge of the truth, there no longer remains a sacrifice for sins, but a certain terrifying expectation of judgment…How much severer punishment do you think he will deserve who has trampled under foot the Son of God, and has regarded as unclean the blood of the covenant by which he was sanctified, and has insulted the Spirit of grace? For we know Him who said, 'Vengeance is Mine, I will repay.' And again, 'The Lord will judge His people.' It is a terrifying thing to fall into the hands of the living God." (Hebrews 10:26-31)

In the second epistle of Peter we read:

"For if after they have escaped the defilements of the world by the knowledge of the Lord and Savior Jesus Christ, they are again entangled in them and are overcome, the last state has become worse for them than the first. For it would be better for them not to have known the way of righteousness, than having known it, to turn away from the holy commandment delivered to them." (II Peter 2:20-21)

And finally, the Apostle John stated:

"The one who says, 'I have come to know Him,' and does not keep His commandments, is a liar, and the truth is not in him. Little children, let no one deceive you; the one who practices righteousness is righteous, just as He is righteous; the one who practices sin is of the devil…No one who is born of God practices sin, because His seed abides in him; and he cannot sin, because he is born of God." (I John 2:4; 3:7-9)

In spite of the overwhelming evidence to the contrary, there are those who simply will not accept what the Bible clearly teaches. Motivated by a false notion of the mercy of God, these well-intentioned teachers wish to open wide the gates of heaven to anyone who gives the slightest commitment to Christianity. However, just because there are some who pass along this perverted, anemic gospel does not make it truth. As Paul stated, "God has not called us for the purpose of impurity, but in sanctification. So, he who rejects *this* is not rejecting man but the God who gives His Holy Spirit to you." (I Thessalonians 4:7-8)

When a woman stands before God with a life of carnality, selfishness, and unrepentant sin, her doctrinal opinions will no longer matter. Her dead faith, which she exercised here on earth, will be exposed for what it is, and she will discover, to her horror, that she has sentenced herself to an everlasting place of torment—HELL!**

One of the key reasons people remain in sin is because they lack a fear of God. Any attempt to override the voice of the Holy Spirit's conviction in a sinner's life is dangerous. Solomon had much to say about the fear of the Lord:

"The fear of the LORD is the beginning of knowledge; fools despise wisdom and instruction." (Proverbs 1:7) "Do not be wise in your own eyes; fear the LORD and turn away from evil." (Proverbs 3:7) "The fear of the LORD prolongs life, but the years of the wicked will be shortened." (Proverbs 10:27) "In the fear of the

---

** We do not mean to infer that one can ever become good enough or do anything to earn her way into heaven. However, the one who has a real, saving faith in God does not remain in habitual sin. She has undergone the genuine repentance discussed in the thirteenth chapter. It does not mean that she will not have struggles; but she has a living, vibrant faith which cannot be held in the shackles of habitual sin.

LORD there is strong confidence, and his children will have refuge. The fear of the LORD is a fountain of life, that one may avoid the snares of death." (Proverbs 14:26-27) "By lovingkindness and truth iniquity is atoned for, and by the fear of the LORD one keeps away from evil." (Proverbs 16:6) "The fear of the LORD leads to life, so that one may sleep satisfied, untouched by evil." (Proverbs 19:23) "Do not let your heart envy sinners, but live in the fear of the LORD always." (Proverbs 23:17)

It is right to fear the Lord. A healthy reverence for God stands as a mighty fortress against the attack of the enemy through temptation.

Grace That Saves From Sin

One of the ways we have gotten off track doctrinally in this century is that there has been a gradual but definite decline in the awareness of the evil nature of sin. Those who have a weak comprehension of the horror of sin will take a weak stand against it. This corporate loss of the shame of sin has been promoted by the "hyper-grace" teachings which have flourished during our time.

When dealing with churchgoing women who are unsaved and/or backslidden, it is important to understand that God's grace is there to empower His people to overcome sin. In fact, one of the prophecies about Jesus was that He would come to "save His people from their sins." (Matthew 1:21)

Maintaining a proper, biblical understanding of God's grace is not a problem unless a woman wishes to cling to her sin. Unfortunately, there are many who do not want to be saved from their sins; they only wish to be saved from hell. In the words of an old-time Baptist preacher, "That's like the unrepentant thief who went before the judge pleading not to be sent to prison. He had no intention of quitting the behavior that got him into his predicament. He only wanted to be spared a prison sentence."

As we mentioned earlier, God has graciously set aside the demands of the law. He now is only looking for confession and repentance from the heart. As stated by the Apostle John, "If we confess our sins, He is faithful and righteous to forgive us our sins and to cleanse us from all unrighteousness." (I John 1:9) Those who imagine that they can remain in unrepentant sin are saying, *"I don't want to be cleansed; I just want to be forgiven."*

William Barclay said the following:

> Grace is not only a gift; it is a grave responsibility. A man cannot go on living the life he lived before he met Jesus Christ. He must be clothed in a new purity and a new holiness and a new goodness. The door is open, but the door is not open to the sinner to come and remain a sinner, but for the sinner to come and become a saint.[5]

Grace Provides an Atmosphere of Acceptance

One of the most important aspects to the grace of God is that it provides a safe haven for the repentant sinner. When a woman in habitual sin repents, she does not need to punish herself further with condemnation. She does not have to earn her way back into the Father's "good graces." When she confesses the wrongness of her actions and turns from them, she is instantly restored.

Jesus expressed this truth in the wonderful story of the prodigal son found in Luke 15. Once he had repented of his sins in the pigpen, he became the immediate recipient of God's grace. One of the most beautiful expositions of the grace illustrated in this story was written by Charles Spurgeon:

His father "ran, and fell on his neck, and kissed him;" — kissed him eagerly. He did not delay a moment; for though he was out of breath, he was not out of love. There stood his son ready to confess his sin; therefore did his father kiss him all the more. The more willing thou art to own thy sin, the more willing is God to forgive thee…

"When he was yet a great way off, his father saw him." It was not with icy eyes that the father looked on his returning son. Love leaped into them, and as he beheld him, he "had compassion on him;" that is, he felt for him. There was no anger in his heart towards his son; he had nothing but pity for his poor boy, who had got into such a pitiable condition. It was true that it was all his own fault, but that did not come before his father's mind…

We read that the father "ran." The compassion of God is followed by swift movements. He is slow to anger, but he is quick to bless. And when he comes, he comes to kiss. What does this much kissing mean? It signifies that, when sinners come to God, he gives them a loving reception, and a hearty welcome. It means much love truly *felt*; for God never gives an expression of love without feeling it in his infinite heart. Oh, how God loves sinners! You who repent, and come to him, will discover how greatly he loves you…

The father's heart is overflowing with gladness, and he cannot restrain his delight. I think he must have shown his joy by *a repeated look*. The father has kissed his son, and he bids him sit down; then he comes in front of him, and looks at him, and feels so happy that he says, "I must give you another kiss," then he walks away a minute; but he is back again before long, saying to himself, "Oh, I must give him another kiss!" He gives him another, for he is so happy. His heart beats fast; he feels very joyful; the old man would like the music to strike up; he wants to be at the dancing; but meanwhile he satisfies himself by a repeated look at his long-lost child. Oh, I believe that God looks at the sinner, and looks at him again, and keeps on looking at him, all the while delighting in the very sight of him, when he is truly repentant, and comes back to his Father's house.[6]

One of the primary aspects of God's grace is that *He will always accept the penitent heart*—no matter how horrendous the sin! From what we have been told, serial killers Ted Bundy and Jeffrey Dahmer both repented and therefore are in heaven this day. When a sinner comes to God in repentance, it does not matter what he or she has done, the slate is wiped CLEAN! No condemnation; no guilt trips. There is only joyful acceptance from God the Father.

Grace Gives the Power to Break Free From Sin

Just as the Apostle Paul was gearing up to deliver his fabulous treatise on righteousness, he made this statement: "…but where sin increased, grace abounded all the more." (Romans 5:20) It is very important for the woman whose life is characterized by lustful acts to know that as much as she has indulged in sin, God has an even greater measure of grace to overcome that sin. As we have already seen, the reason Jesus came was to break the power of sin over the believer's life. Paul said it this way: "For the grace of God that brings salvation has appeared to all men. It teaches us to say 'No' to ungodliness and worldly passions, and to live self-controlled, upright and godly lives in this present age." (Titus 2:11-12 NIV)

Yes, it is true: grace is the means whereby salvation is

available to all of mankind. Yet, it is even more than that. Grace is also a teacher, and its primary subject of instruction is how to live a life pleasing to God. When that temptation arises for something ungodly, grace is there to teach us to say "No." When an opportunity comes to give over to some worldly passion, grace instructs us to deny it. Not only does it help us during those times of temptation, but God's daily grace is an active force in the life of the believer "to live self-controlled, upright and godly lives in this present age."

It is exactly what Paul spoke of when he said, "No temptation has overtaken you but such as is common to man; and God is faithful, who will not allow you to be tempted beyond what you are able, but with the temptation will provide the way of escape also, that you may be able to endure it." (I Corinthians 10:13) It is God's grace that empowers us to withstand the overwhelming desire for sin. In other words, *the atmosphere that provides acceptance and forgiveness when we repent, is the same godly atmosphere which provides a way through every temptation to sin.*

It is my (Steve's) testimony that for the past 20-plus years it has been God's grace that has kept me from giving in to the powerful lust for women that once dominated my life. Just to give one example of the many I could share, I will tell of an incident that happened to me in 1988. At that time, I had only been out of habitual sin for three years. I was in Texas holding a conference on the subject of overcoming sexual addiction. There was an attractive female doctor there who seemed very interested in Pure Life Ministries. She was asking a number of questions and seemed reluctant to leave after the conference.

The man whom I was traveling with had other appointments and asked her to give me a ride back to the house where we were staying. I did not think anything of it at the time. She seemed to have an interest in becoming involved with PLM, so I was glad to have the opportunity to talk with her further. During the drive across town though, I started becoming aware of her physically. When we arrived at the house, I felt an overwhelming lust for her overtake my mind. As I was experiencing this intoxicating desire for her, she made it clear to me that she was available. Just then, at that critical moment, even more overpowering than the lust came a fear that I would get caught if I committed adultery. This all-encompassing fear was all I needed to get out of the situation.

What an example of God's wonderful, sustaining grace! Had I been left to myself, I would have thrown away all that the Lord had accomplished in my life over the previous three years. I would have shattered the trust that had been so painstakingly reestablished with my wife. I would have ruined Pure Life Ministries before it even got off the ground. Indeed, I would have plummeted into the depths of sin once more. Nevertheless, I was not left to myself! God's grace was there to provide a way of escape.

If His grace is there for the believer, why do some continually cave in to their temptations? I believe it is because they do not learn the secret of abiding in His presence. As John said, "And you know that He appeared in order to take away sins; and in Him there is no sin. No one who abides in Him sins...And the one who keeps His commandments abides in Him, and He in him." (I John 3:5-6,24)

Allow me (Steve) to illustrate how this works in a practical way. In Heathrow Airport outside of London, there is a moving walkway that goes right down the middle of the terminal for probably a half-mile. There are various shops, restaurants, and bars lining each side. If a person wishes to find sin, it is there for the taking.

Using that airport as an illustration of the Christian journey of life, the escalator would be the object which would represent God's grace. As I abide in Christ, it somehow keeps me safe from all the temptations and trappings of this world. My responsibility is to stay attached to the Vine; God's job is to empower me to overcome the temptations of life that come along. Maintaining a dependent relationship upon the Lord every day through prayer and Bible study keeps me securely attached to the Vine and spiritually nourished. These are the mediums which the Lord uses to infuse His power into my life.

The moving walkway is an illustration of God's grace transporting me through the hellish enticements found in this world. It is not my own self-effort that is getting me through. I am simply standing on the moving sidewalk of God's grace. It is His grace that is carrying me through. He will receive all of the glory when I arrive in heaven.

Yes, if I were bent on committing sin, I could climb over the escalator handrail at any moment during my transit and could go into a bookstore that offers pornography. Yet, there is a spiritual handrail called the fear of the Lord which operates as a boundary within me. It is an added, protective feature built into me which is just enough of a barrier to keep me from wandering toward the ever-present allurements provided by the spirit of the world. Those whose fear of God has been paralyzed by the teachings of "sloppy grace" do not enjoy this added protection. In even worse trouble are those who wander around free of the discipline and spiritual strength that comes through maintaining a daily devotional life. They must fight the battle of temptation in their own strength—a battle sure to be lost.

I have a better understanding of His wonderful grace because I have been kept by it for a long time. I have seen it at work on my behalf many times over the years. Earlier in my walk with the Lord, I did not understand grace so well. In fact, as astonishing as it may seem when considering the depth of sin that I had once been involved in, I became quite a Pharisee when I first started walking in victory over sexual sin. I gave myself much undeserved credit for my freedom. I became remarkably similar to the Pharisee in Luke eighteen who said, "God, I thank Thee that I am not like other people: swindlers, unjust, adulterers, or even like this tax-gatherer. I fast twice a week; I pay tithes of all that I get." (Luke 18:11-12) I was continually comparing myself favorably to others. Just like this Pharisee, I was doing many things right. My zeal for the Lord was intense. I was willing to live a "sold-out" life for God, sacrificing everything else to serve Him. My devotional life was firmly in place, but I had lost sight of what a wretch I had been and all that the Lord had done for me. I had become very prideful and self-righteous.

God continued dealing with me. He was unwilling to leave me in such a terrible state. One day in 1991, the Lord helped me in a quite unexpected way. I was due to make an appearance on *Focus on the Family* the following week. I was preparing to share my testimony on this program, knowing that perhaps millions of people would hear it. Deep down inside I was anxious to share with the world how *I* had overcome sexual sin. God will share His glory with no other, however.

During that time, I was preaching in various churches around the country. This particular weekend, I was scheduled to hold services in a church in Michigan. We live in Kentucky, and normally Kathy would travel with me on such a trip, but she had developed a backache and decided to stay home. I would have to make the six-hour drive by myself. There was no lack of confidence within me.

I made the long drive that day, struggling at times with the temptation to go into some city and look for pornography, or worse. But I managed to quell those incessant thoughts and made it into Michigan. After filling up my gas tank at a truck stop, I went into the store to use their restroom. Making my way through the store (to properly appreciate what happened next, it might be helpful to imagine me walking through in all my pharisaical garb!), I noticed a man standing at the magazine rack looking at a porn magazine. I walked by him, peering over his shoulder hoping to see flesh. Sure enough, the magazine was opened to a centerfold layout of some chosen beauty for that month.

That one glimpse of flesh haunted me all weekend. Somehow, I made it through Sunday services and on Monday morning I started home for Kentucky. As soon as I left the parsonage, my mind quickly drifted back to that truck stop. "No! I will not stop and look at that magazine!" I exclaimed to myself. No matter how strong of a stance I tried to take, the picture of the girl continued to plague me. I eventually reached the sign indicating that the off-ramp was one mile away. "I will not stop! I am going on with God!" I shouted. "Glory, hallelujah!"

When the turn-off appeared, I exited the freeway, drove straight to that gas station, went in and saturated my mind with the pictures in that magazine. My heart was thumping wildly as I scrambled through the pages. Just then, a tiny voice inside me yelled, "Run!"

Knowing it to be the Holy Spirit, I left immediately and made the long, guilt-filled trip back to Kentucky. For the next several days, I continually berated myself. One morning, my self-condemnation reached its peak. "How could you be so stupid! Here you are about to go on national radio, and you have looked at pornography! Stupid!" On and on the self-imposed tirade went.

Before finishing the story, I must refer to an incident that happened to me ten years prior. I was a cadet in the Los Angeles Sheriff's Academy. The 18-week training was drawing to a close. I was one of the fortunate ones who had endured the rigorous academy. A third of the class of one hundred and fifty cadets had dropped out. Those of us who made it lived in a certain degree of fear of doing anything that might cause us to be disqualified.

This particular day the cadets were bussed out to the

Pomona Fair Grounds to participate in a two-day intensive driving school. There was a high-speed course that was set up with orange parking cones in the vast asphalt area. My turn finally arrived. The first thing I noticed about the squad car was that it was equipped with a roll cage. A helmet sat on the driving seat awaiting me. "Get in, put on your helmet and take off," said the fearless instructor sitting in the passenger seat.

I did exactly what I was told. I was driving fairly fast when, to my surprise, the instructor yelled out, "Faster!" I immediately responded by increasing my speed even more. I was flying around the curves and accelerating on the straight-a-ways. Coming to one particularly difficult curve, I lost control for a second and was forced to drive off of the track. I immediately barreled through the cones again, getting back on the roadway and finished out the course. I sat in silence as the instructor filled out his paperwork. Knowing I had gotten off of the track, I moaned, "I guess I failed the course." I was sick inside thinking it might affect my graduating the academy.

"Failed? Why do you think you failed?" he asked.

"I missed that turn and drove right off the track," I lamented.

"Yeah, but you jumped right back on! You did great!" He exclaimed.

Ten years later, as I was on my morning prayer-walk, beating myself for viewing the pornography in the gas station, God spoke to me. (Tears well up in my eyes all these years later as I recall this incident.) In one of those crisp, eternal moments, I relived the incident that occurred a decade before in the squad car. Now it was the Lord speaking. "Steve, you made one little mistake. But you've been doing great! You've been in prayer everyday. You've been pressing in to Me. You've been in the

Word faithfully. Yes, you got off track for a moment, but you jumped right back on!"

I had come into a true revelation about the grace of God. From that day on, I understood that my victory over sin was not because of my efforts but because of God's fabulous grace!

ADDENDUM

PURE LIFE MINISTRIES WEBSITE SURVEY RESULTS

1. Which of the following types of behavior regarding romance, past or present, are you involved in? Select all that apply.

	Respondents	Percentage*
17 & Younger (35 respondents)		
Entertaining romantic fantasies:	23	66%
Reading romance novels:	9	26%
Watching soap operas:	5	14%
Establishing romantic relationships on the Internet:	5	14%
Flirting with guys:	19	54%
Frequent casual dating:	2	6%
Watching romantic movies:	17	49%
18-24 (172 respondents)		
Entertaining romantic fantasies:	141	82%
Reading romance novels:	60	35%
Watching soap operas:	31	18%
Establishing romantic relationships on the Internet:	39	23%
Flirting with guys:	86	50%
Frequent casual dating:	26	15%
Watching romantic movies:	100	58%
25-34 (150 respondents)		
Entertaining romantic fantasies:	109	73%
Reading romance novels:	36	24%
Watching soap operas:	43	29%
Establishing romantic relationships on the Internet:	27	18%
Flirting with guys:	54	36%
Frequent casual dating:	24	16%
Watching romantic movies:	84	56%
35+ (118 respondents)		
Entertaining romantic fantasies:	72	61%
Reading romance novels:	32	27%
Watching soap operas:	30	25%

	Respondents	Percentage*
35+ (118 respondents), *cont'd.*		
Establishing romantic relationships on the Internet:	16	14%
Flirting with guys:	33	28%
Frequent casual dating:	14	12%
Watching romantic movies:	54	46%
All Women (475 respondents)		
Entertaining romantic fantasies:	345	73%
Reading romance novels:	137	29%
Watching soap operas:	109	23%
Establishing romantic relationships on the Internet:	87	18%
Flirting with guys:	192	40%
Frequent casual dating:	66	14%
Watching romantic movies:	255	54%

2. Which of the following types of behavior regarding pornography, past or present, have you been involved in? Select all that apply.

17 & Younger (35 respondents)

Viewing adult movies with another person:	5	14%
Viewing adult movies alone:	21	60%
Occasionally viewing magazines/Internet porn:	19	54%
Regularly viewing magazines/Internet porn:	12	34%
Reading pornographic stories:	20	57%

18-24 (172 respondents)

Viewing adult movies with another person:	26	15%
Viewing adult movies alone:	80	47%
Occasionally viewing magazines/Internet porn:	91	53%
Regularly viewing magazines/Internet porn:	45	26%
Reading pornographic stories:	95	55%

25-34 (150 respondents)

Viewing adult movies with another person:	56	37%
Viewing adult movies alone:	68	45%
Occasionally viewing magazines/Internet porn:	89	59%
Regularly viewing magazines/Internet porn:	21	14%
Reading pornographic stories:	66	44%

	Respondents	Percentage*
35+ (118 respondents)		
Viewing adult movies with another person:	48	41%
Viewing adult movies alone:	43	36%
Occasionally viewing magazines/Internet porn:	52	44%
Regularly viewing magazines/Internet porn:	13	11%
Reading pornographic stories:	39	33%
All Women (475 respondents)		
Viewing adult movies with another person:	135	28%
Viewing adult movies alone:	212	45%
Occasionally viewing magazines/Internet porn:	251	53%
Regularly viewing magazines/Internet porn:	91	19%
Reading pornographic stories:	220	46%

3. Which of the following types of behavior regarding sexual sin, past or present, have you been involved in? Select all that apply.

17 & Younger (35 respondents)		
Masturbation:	32	91%
On-line sexual conversations:	10	29%
Promiscuity/fornication with other singles:	5	14%
Affair(s):	0	0%
Straight but having bisexual experiences:	5	14%
Homosexual lifestyle:	1	3%
Involved in the adult entertainment industry:	0	0%

18-24 (172 respondents)		
Masturbation:	157	91%
On-line sexual conversations:	73	42%
Promiscuity/fornication with other singles:	52	30%
Affair(s):	5	3%
Straight but having bisexual experiences:	27	16%
Homosexual lifestyle:	5	3%
Involved in the adult entertainment industry:	5	3%

25-34 (150 respondents)		
Masturbation:	138	92%
On-line sexual conversations:	46	31%

	Respondents	Percentage*
25-34 (150 respondents), *cont'd.*		
Promiscuity/fornication with other singles:	62	41%
Affair(s):	21	14%
Straight but having bisexual experiences:	29	19%
Homosexual lifestyle:	6	4%
Involved in the adult entertainment industry:	6	4%
35+ (118 respondents)		
Masturbation:	102	86%
On-line sexual conversations:	23	19%
Promiscuity/fornication with other singles:	52	44%
Affair(s):	29	25%
Straight but having bisexual experiences:	14	12%
Homosexual lifestyle:	4	3%
Involved in the adult entertainment industry:	5	4%
All Women (475 respondents)		
Masturbation:	429	90%
On-line sexual conversations:	152	32%
Promiscuity/fornication with other singles:	171	36%
Affair(s):	55	12%
Straight but having bisexual experiences:	75	16%
Homosexual lifestyle:	16	3%
Involved in the adult entertainment industry:	16	3%

4. Were you ever sexually molested by an older person as a child?

17 & Younger (35 respondents)		
Yes	7	20%
No	28	80%
18-24 (161 respondents)		
Yes	38	24%
No	123	76%
25-34 (130 respondents)		
Yes	53	41%
No	77	59%

	Respondents	Percentage*
35+ (84 respondents)		
Yes	38	45%
No	46	55%
All Women (410 respondents)		
Yes	136	33%
No	274	67%

5. Which best describes you?

17 & Younger (35 respondents)

I have complete victory over past struggles:	6	17%
I still occasionally struggle but am doing fairly well:	17	49%
I still struggle regularly:	12	34%

18-24 (172 respondents)

I have complete victory over past struggles:	19	11%
I still occasionally struggle but am doing fairly well:	108	63%
I still struggle regularly:	44	26%

25-34 (150 respondents)

I have complete victory over past struggles:	30	20%
I still occasionally struggle but am doing fairly well:	85	57%
I still struggle regularly:	36	24%

35+ (118 respondents)

I have complete victory over past struggles:	28	24%
I still occasionally struggle but am doing fairly well:	58	49%
I still struggle regularly:	32	27%

All Women (475 respondents)

I have complete victory over past struggles:	83	17%
I still occasionally struggle but am doing fairly well:	268	56%
I still struggle regularly:	124	26%

* Percentages may not total 100% due to rounding or because respondents were able to choose more than one option.

CONCLUSIONS

By design, this brief survey was not intended to be rigidly scientific, and these statistics cannot be applied to the general population of women. However, there are a number of assumptions and noteworthy trends which can be derived from these statistics.

- There is a clear dropping off in the tendency to flirt as a woman grows older: over 50% of those under age 25, while only 28% of those over age 35, admit to doing this behavior.

- Only 15% of girls under the age of 25 acknowledged viewing adult movies with another person, while 39% of women over 25 admitted to this. By contrast, 48% of girls under 25 said that they watched X-rated movies alone, while this number dropped to 36% of women over 35 years of age.

- Regular viewers of magazines and/or Internet porn progressively drops as the respondents' age increases: under 17, 34%; 18-24, 26%; 25-34, 14%; and over 35, 11%.

- Masturbation (around 90%), bisexuality (around 16%) and homosexuality (around 3%) levels remained fairly consistent for all age ranges.

- As one might guess, the number of women who admit to having affairs rises dramatically through the age groups: under 17, 0%; 18-24, 3%; 25-34, 14%; and over 35, 25%.

- And finally, the pattern of women who were molested as children follows the same upward trend: under 17, 20%; 18-24, 24%; 25-34, 41%; and over 35, 45%. This would make sense considering how the public awareness of this problem has grown over the past 20 years.

NOTES

CHAPTER ONE

1. Jerry Ropelato, "Pornography Statistics 2007" *Internet Filter Review*, accessed online at: http://internet-filter-review.toptenreviews.com/internet-pornography-statistics.html.
2. Ramona Richards, "Dirty Little Secret" *Today's Christian Woman*, (Sept/Oct 2003).
3. Jerry Ropelato.
4. Jason Collum, "A Woman's Struggle, Too" *AFA Journal*, (March 2004) accessed online at http://www.afajournal.org/2004/March/304pornography.asp.
5. www.washingtonpost.com (September 15, 2005).
6. *Ibid.*
7. *Ibid.*

CHAPTER TWO

1. Brook Wayne, "Of Princes and Fairytale Dreams: Fostering Emotional Purity in Teenage Girls" *Unchained!*, a Pure Life Ministries publication (Summer 2002). For more of her writing, please go to www.wisgate.com.
2. Kay Arthur, *Lord, I Want to Know You*, (Colorado Springs, CO: WaterBrook Press, 2000) p. 35.
3. *Ibid.*, p. 36.
4. Nancy Leigh DeMoss, *Lies Women Believe and the Truth that Sets Them Free*, (Chicago: Moody Publishers, 2001) pps. 194-195.
5. *Ibid.*, pps. 197, 200-201.

CHAPTER THREE

1. Tammy Tibbitts, "Plastic Surgery Stats" *Jane* (June 5, 2006), accessed online at: http://www.janemag.com.
2. *Ibid.*
3. Dr. Phil, "Teen Plastic Surgery" *Tapes and Transcripts* (October 13, 2006), available at www.tapesandtranscripts.drphil.com.
4. American Academy of Pediatrics, Committee on Public Education, "Sexuality, Contraception, and the Media" *Pediatrics*, Vol. 107, No. 1 (January 2001), accessed online at http://aappolicy.aappublications.org/cgi/reprint/pediatrics;107/1/191.pdf.
5. *Ibid.*

6. Laura Meckler, "Survey: Teens Feel Pressured to Have Sex" *Associated Press* (May 20, 2003), accessed online at http://findarticles.com/p/articles/mi_qn4196/is_20030520/ai_n10883646.

7. The Kaiser Family Foundation, "Sex on TV: Content and Context" as quoted by John Kiesewetter and Richelle Thompson, "TV's Sex Content Climbs Study Says" *Cincinnati Enquirer* (February 7, 2001).

8. *Ibid.*

9. William D. Mosher, Anjani Chandra & Jo Jones, "Sexual Behavior and Selected Health Measures: Men and Women 15–44 Years of Age, United States, 2002" *Advance Data from Vital and Health Statistics*, No. 362 (September 15, 2005), accessed online at http://www.cdc.gov/nchs/data/ad/ad362.pdf.

10. London School of Economics (January 2002) as cited by Mike Genung, "Getting to the Roots of the Porn Epidemic" accessed online at: http://www.crosswalk.com/1457170/.

11. Much of this section was extrapolated from Steve Gallagher's book, *Irresistible to God* (Dry Ridge, KY: Pure Life Ministries, 2003).

12. David Sherman, "What Does a Manager Do?" (testimony before the Michigan House Ethics and Constitutional Law Committee, January 2000), as archived at http://www.americandecency.org/main.php?f=issues/pornography/managerDo. David Sherman has since recanted his testimony, and apparently has returned to his lifestyle. However, we have quoted his words intact, as we believe he was telling the truth.

13. Shelley Lubben, "The Truth Behind the Fantasy of Porn" accessed at http://www.shelleylubben.com/articles/thetruth.pdf.

14. *Ibid.*

15. Bob Harrington, *The Chaplain of Bourbon Street*, (Nashville, TN: Impact Books, 1969) pps. 124-126.

16. C.S. Lewis, *The Great Divorce*, (San Francisco: Harper, 1946) pps. 78-79.

CHAPTER FOUR

1. *Strong's Exhaustive Concordance of the Bible* (Peabody, MA: Hendrickson Publishers, 1988).

2. *The Bible Dictionary* (Norwalk CT: Easton Press, 1995).

3. *International Standard Bible Encyclopedia* (Grand Rapids, MI: Wm. B. Eerdmans Publishing Co.).

CHAPTER FIVE

1. Frank Worthen, *Love in Action Newsletter* (January, 1983) p. 46.

2. Ronald A. Jenson, *Biblical Meditation* (Oakland, CA: I.C.B.I. Press, 1982) p. 39.
3. Dietrich Bonhoeffer, *Temptation* (London, England: SCM Press, 1964) p. 33.
4. Adam Clarke, *Clarke's Commentary on the Old Testament* as cited in AGES Digital Library (Rio, WI: AGES Software, Inc., 2001) p. 1694.

CHAPTER SIX
1. Rape, Abuse & Incest National Network (RAINN), "Statistics: The Facts About Rape" accessed at http://www.rainn.org/statistics/index.html.
2. *Ibid.*
3. *Ibid.*
4. Rape, Abuse & Incest National Network (RAINN), "Statistics: The Victims of Sexual Assault" accessed at http://www.rainn.org/statistics/victims-of-sexual-assault.html.
5. David Finkelhor et al, as quoted in "Statistics: Child Sexual Abuse and Assault" *Rape & Sexual Abuse Center*, accessed at http://www.rasac.org/education/statistics.html#01.
6. FBI Law Enforcement Bulletin, as quoted in "Child Molester Statistics" *Yello Dyno*, accessed at http://www.yellodyno.com/html/child_molester_stats.html.
7. Forward, 1993.
8. Nancy DeMoss, pps. 68-70.
9. A.W. Tozer, as cited in Warren Wiersbe, *The Best of A.W. Tozer* (Grand Rapids, MI: Baker Publishing House, 1978) p. 176.
10. Andrew Murray, *Humility* (New Kensington, PA: Whitaker House, 1982) pps. 24, 12.

CHAPTER SEVEN
1. J.C. Ryle, *Holiness* (Darlington, England: Evangelical Press, 1879) p. 7.

CHAPTER TEN
1. *Fausset's Bible Dictionary* as cited in AGES Digital Library (Grand Rapids, MI: Zondervan, 1984) as cited in AGES Digital Library (Rio, WI: AGES Software, Inc., 2001) p. 859.
2. Charles Hodge, *Commentary On the Epistle to the Romans* (Wm. B. Eerdmans Publishing Company, 1984) as cited in AGES Digital Library (Rio, WI: AGES Software, Inc. 2001) p. 359.
3. Nelson E. Hinman, sermon recording: "Never Beyond What's Written" (Sacramento, CA: Heart Talk Ministry).

CHAPTER ELEVEN

1. George Barna, *Real Teens: A Contemporary Snapshot of Youth Culture* (Ventura, CA: Regal Books, 2001).
2. Erwin W. Lutzer, *Living With Your Passions* (Wheaton, IL: Victor Books, 1983) p. 31.
3. Lester Sumrall, *60 Things God Said About Sex* (New York, NY: Thomas Publishers, 1981) p. 53.
4. A. W. Tozer, as quoted in Wiersbe, pps. 85-86.
5. David Wilkerson, *Set The Trumpet To Thy Mouth* (Lindale, TX: World Challenge, Inc, 1985) pps. 53-55.
6. Ronald A. Jenson, pps. 15-18.
7. Donald E. Wildmon, *The Home Invaders* (Wheaton, IL: Victor Books, 1985) pps. 45-46.
8. *Webster's New Collegiate Dictionary* (Springfield, MA: G. & C. Merriam Co., 1960).

CHAPTER TWELVE

1. Merrill F. Unger, *Demons in the World Today* (Wheaton, IL: Tyndale House, 1971) pps. 113-114.
2. *Ibid.*
3. Merlin A. Carothers, *What's On Your Mind?* (Escondido, CA: The Foundation of Praise, 1984) pps. 12-13, 17-18.

CHAPTER FOURTEEN

1. *Baker Encyclopedia of the Bible, Vol. 1*, edited by Walter A. Elwell (Grand Rapids, MI: Baker Book House, 1988) p. 631.
2. Leonard Ravenhill, *Revival Praying*, (Minneapolis, MN: Bethany House Publishers, 1962) p. 40.

CHAPTER FIFTEEN

1. Ronald A. Jenson, pps. 15-18.

CHAPTER SIXTEEN

1. Oswald Chambers, as cited in *Oswald Chambers The Best From All His Books*, edited by Harry Verploegh (Nashville, TN: Thomas Nelson, Inc., 1989) p. 204.

CHAPTER SEVENTEEN

1. W.E. Vine, *VINE'S Expository Dictionary of Old and New Testament Words* (Nashville, TN: Thomas Nelson Publishers, 1996) p. 684.

2. Matthew Henry as cited in *The Bethany Parallel Commentary on the New Testament* (Minneapolis, MN: Bethany House Publishers, 1983) p. 1029.

3. *Theological Dictionary of the New Testament*, edited by Gerhard Kittel and Gerhard Friedrich (Grand Rapids, MI: Wm. B. Eerdmans Publishing Co., 1976) p. 550.

4. John F. MacArthur, Jr., *The Gospel According to Jesus* (Panorama City, CA: Word of Grace, 1988) p. 60.

5. William Barclay, as cited in Michael L. Brown, *Go and Sin No More: A Call to Holiness* (Ventura, CA: Gospel Light Publications, 2000) p. 224.

6. C.H. Spurgeon, "Many Kisses for Returning Sinners", a Sermon delivered at the Metropolitan Tabernacle, Newington, England (March 29, 1891), accessed at http://www.spurgeon.org/sermons/2236.htm.

OTHER BOOKS AVAILABLE BY PURE LIFE MINISTRIES

WHEN HIS SECRET SIN BREAKS YOUR HEART

What can be more devastating for a wife than to discover her husband has a secret obsession with pornography and other women? Yet, this is what countless Christian wives face every day. Kathy Gallagher has been there; she understands the pain of rejection, the feelings of hopelessness and the questions that plague a hurting wife.

In this collection of letters, Kathy imparts heart-felt encouragement by providing the practical, biblical answers that helped her find healing in the midst of her most trying storm. The 30-day journal offers wives a place to prayerfully reflect and meditate upon Kathy's letters.

A BIBLICAL GUIDE TO COUNSELING THE SEXUAL ADDICT

A SERIOUS book for Christian Counselors
Christian men scoping pornography…
Adulterous eyes in the pulpit…
Casual sex among singles…
Now, more than ever, the Church needs godly people willing to passionately impart biblical truths to those drowning in the cesspool of sexual idolatry. Tackle the tough issues with this practical guide gleaned from 20 years of experience!

INTOXICATED WITH BABYLON

Intoxicated With Babylon is by far Steve Gallagher's best writing; its strength is his sobering deliverance of the unvarnished truth to a Church rife with sensuality and worldly compromise. In a time when evangelical Christians seem content to be lulled to sleep by the spirit of Antichrist, *Intoxicated With Babylon* sounds a clarion wake-up call in an effort to draw the Body of Christ back to the Cross and holy living. Those with itching ears will find no solace here, but sincere believers will experience deep repentance and a fresh encounter with the Living God.

OUT OF THE DEPTHS OF SEXUAL SIN

A Cop. A Big City. A Secret Obsession with Sex.
was an aggressive deputy on the Los Angeles Sheriff's Department... but he had a dark secret. Behind the arrogant exterior was a man obsessed with the triple-X-rated underworld. Could God really bring something good out of a life so ravaged by sin? This book is the riveting story of a man who courageously battled his way out of deep darkness to pioneer Pure Life Ministries—the first ministry in the world to help men find freedom from sexual addiction.

Not your typical *"sinner-gets-saved-and-lives-happily-ever-after"* book.

FOR MORE RESOURCES VISIT US ONLINE AT WWW.PURELIFEMINISTRIES.ORG

WHETHER USED INDIVIDUALLY OR COLLECTIVELY, EACH OF THESE BIBLE STUDIES IS A GREAT TOOL FOR PERSONAL GROWTH OR GROUP DISCIPLESHIP.

THE WALK OF REPENTANCE

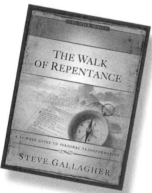

A 24-week Bible study for the Christian who desires to be more deeply consecrated to God. Each week addresses the everyday challenges believers face. Experience the times of spiritual refreshing that follow repentance; go deeper in God as you allow His Word to take root in your heart.

A LAMP UNTO MY FEET

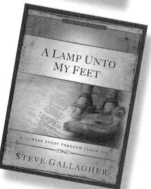

A Lamp unto My Feet is a 12-week journey through the beautiful Psalm 119, and a great resource for any individual seeking guidance in the midst of life's struggles. At each week's end, they will also read about the life of David, a man after God's own heart and author of this epic psalm. Every reader will be brought into a deeper love, respect and appreciation for God's Word.

PRESSING ON TOWARD THE HEAVENLY CALLING

The Prison Epistles are a divine archive of profound revelations about the kingdom of God. Ephesians, Philippians and Colossians all offer incredible glimpses into the heavenly domain inhabited by God. *Pressing On Toward the Heavenly Calling* is a 12-week study that will challenge you to reach for the abundant life in God that Paul testifies is available to every one of us.

TO ORDER VISIT OUR WEB SITE OR CALL TOLL FREE 888.PURELIFE

Pure Life Ministries helps Christian men achieve lasting freedom from sexual sin. The Apostle Paul said, "Walk in the Spirit and you will not fulfill the lust of the flesh." Since 1986, Pure Life Ministries (PLM) has been discipling men into the holiness and purity of heart that comes from a Spirit-controlled life. At the root, illicit sexual behavior is sin and must be treated with spiritual remedies. Our counseling programs and teaching materials are rooted in the biblical principles that, when applied to the believer's daily life, will lead him out of bondage and into freedom in Christ.

BIBLICAL TEACHING MATERIALS
Pure Life offers a full line of books, audiotapes and videotapes specifically designed to give men the tools they need to live in sexual purity.

RESIDENTIAL CARE
The most intense and involved counseling PLM offers comes through the **Live-in Program** (6-12 months), in Dry Ridge, Kentucky. The godly and sober atmosphere on our 45-acre campus provokes the hunger for God and deep repentance that destroys the hold of sin in men's lives.

HELP AT HOME
The **Overcomers At Home Program** (OCAH) is available for those who cannot come to Kentucky for the Live-in program. This twelve-week counseling program features weekly counseling sessions and many of the same teachings offered in the Live-in Program.

CARE FOR WIVES
Pure Life Ministries also offers help to wives of men in sexual sin. Our wives' counselors have suffered through the trials and storms of such a discovery and can offer a devastated wife a sympathetic ear and the biblical solutions that worked in their lives.

PURE LIFE MINISTRIES
14 School St. • Dry Ridge • KY • 41035
Office: 859.824.4444 • Orders: 888.293.8714
info@purelifeministries.org
www.purelifeministries.org